Who Will Cleanse from Postbaptismal Sins?

Who Will Cleanse from Postbaptismal Sins?

Bishops and Forgiveness from Postbaptismal Sins AD 250 to 391

DAVID W. T. BRATTSTON

WIPF & STOCK · Eugene, Oregon

WHO WILL CLEANSE FROM POSTBAPTISMAL SINS?
Bishops and Forgiveness from Postbaptismal Sins AD 250 to 391

Wipf & Stock
An Imprint of Wipf and Stock Publishers
199 W. 8th Ave., Suite 3
Eugene, OR 97401

www.wipfandstock.com

PAPERBACK ISBN: 979-8-3852-7778-0
HARDCOVER ISBN: 979-8-3852-7779-7
EBOOK ISBN: 979-8-3852-7780-3

VERSION NUMBER 04/28/26

The book's title is in reference to Gregory of Nazianzus, "Concerning Himself and the Bishops," lines 486–87, in *Three Poems*, 64.

DEDICATED TO

Steve Campanelli, Joseph Cochran,
Patrick Burke, and Gary Yemen

Contents

Abstract

THE QUESTIONS STUDIED IN this present thesis are in the period of the priests penitentiary (250 CE to 391 CE) among Christians in the Roman Empire:

- whether there was pardon for any sins committed after water baptism;
- whether all sins were considered remissible after baptism, or were there exceptions;
- which actions constituted an appropriate manifestation of sorrow and remorse for sins; and
- which officers of the church held authority to hear and adjudicate confessions of sins and declare them forgiven on earth and in heaven.

After examining primary sources, the thesis concludes that all of these questions were decided by the local bishop or his diocesan or parish council.

Abbreviations

ANF — *The Ante-Nicene Fathers: Translations of the Writings of the Fathers Down to A.D. 325*. Edited by Alexander Roberts and James Donaldson. 10 vols. 1885–1887. American reprint edited by A. Cleveland Coxe. Grand Rapids: Eerdmans, 1986.

NPNF 1 — *A Select Library of Nicene and Post-Nicene Fathers of the Christian Church*. Series 1. 14 vols. 1886–1889. Edited by Philip Schaff. Grand Rapids: Eerdmans, 1994.

NPNF 2 — *A Select Library of Nicene and Post-Nicene Fathers of the Christian Church*. Series 2. 14 vols. Edited by Philip Schaff and Henry Wace. Grand Rapids: Eerdmans, 1983.

Introduction

ANANIAS AND SAPPHIRA

THE FIRST RECORDED CASE of Christians sinning after baptism, and its consequences, is in Acts 5:5–10:

> 5 But a man named Ananias, with the consent of his wife Sapphira, sold a piece of property; 2 with his wife's knowledge, he kept back some of the proceeds and brought only a part and laid it at the apostles' feet. 3 "Ananias," Peter asked, "why has Satan filled your heart to lie to the Holy Spirit and to keep back part of the proceeds of the land? 4 While it remained unsold, did it not remain your own? And after it was sold, were not the proceeds at your disposal? How is it that you have contrived this deed in your heart? You did not lie to us but to God!" 5 Now when Ananias heard these words, he fell down and died. And great fear seized all who heard of it. 6 The young men came and wrapped up his body, then carried him out and buried him. 7 After an interval of about three hours his wife came in, not knowing what had happened. 8 Peter said to her, "Tell me whether you and your husband sold the land for such and such a price." And she said, "Yes, that was the price." 9 Then Peter said to her, "How is it that you have agreed together to put the Spirit of the Lord to the test? Look, the feet of those who have buried your husband are at the door, and they will carry you out." 10 Immediately she fell down

> at his feet and died. When the young men came in they found her dead, so they carried her out and buried her beside her husband.

A multitude of church fathers before the fifth century referred to the incidents of Ananias and Sapphira without commenting whether their treatment was too severe, bad or good, or in any way instructive as to repentance and forgiveness.[1] They simply accepted the pericope at face value.

Contrary to what today's Christians might expect, many early fathers approved of the killing of these first two postbaptismal sinners and did not criticize the death sentence in their case. Despite his general laxity—even nonchalance—in dealing with postbaptismal sins, John Chrysostom approved more than the other fathers. Chrysostom characterized the death penalty here as "right thinking, solicitude, good management"[2] and the sin it punished as "an example of extreme lawbreaking, infringing the commandment right from the outset."[3] He also preached "for even if they stole their own money, nevertheless the deed was sacrilege."[4] His "Homily 12" on the Lukan Acts characterizes as "sacrilege"[5] and expands: "How many evils grow out of the sacrilege: covetousness, contempt of God, impiety."[6] Chrysostom addresses Acts 5 in an argument that sins unpunished in this life will be punished in hell,

1. Ambrose, *Explanatio Psalmorvm XII* 36.24; Ambrose, *Expositio Psalmi CXVIII* 18.7; Ambrose, *Repentance* 2.9; Ambrose, *Three Books of St. Ambrose* 3.9; Ambrosiaster, *Questions on Old and New*, questions 58 and 97; Basil, *Herewith Begins the Morals* 11.3; Chrysostom, *Commentary on the Psalms*, Ps 7; Chrysostom, *De laudibus sancti Pauli* 1–7.10; Mitchell, *Heavenly Trumpet*; Chrysostom, *Acts of the Apostles* 21, 33; Chrysostom, *First Epistle of Paul* 14.4; Chrysostom, *Second Epistle of Paul* 29; Clement, *Stromata* 1.154; Cyril, *Catechetical Lectures* 6.27; Archelaus, *Disputation with Manes*; Gregory of Nazianzus, *Carmina Theologica A*; Gregory of Nazianzus, *Oration* 34; Tertullian, *On Modesty* 21.

2. Chrysostom, *Commentary on the Psalms*, Ps 4, 1:59.

3. Chrysostom, *Commentary on the Psalms*, Ps 6, 1:99.

4. Chrysostom, *Beginning of Acts* 3.5 (Compton, 288).

5. Chrysostom, "Homily 12," *Acts of the Apostles* (*NPNF* 1 11:77–78).

6. Chrysostom, "Homily 12," *Acts of the Apostles* (*NPNF* 1 11:79).

and Christians must not take comfort that they have "gotten away" with some trespasses: "Ananias and Sapphira were immediately punished, because they stole part of what they had offered."[7]

Although admitting the death penalty for sin was inflicted only twice in the Bible, counting Ananias and Sapphira as only once,[8] Chrysostom preached this of their sin: "The deed does not admit of pardon, it is past pleading for."[9] *Contra Novatianum* merely notes the following in passing: "The law, whose greater severity had been motivated by the fragility of the human race, not only softened this rigor, but was a proof of gentleness and goodness, and the law of mercy was severe in punishment."[10] In addition, Chrysostom wrote that "deep fear had to be instilled into the others,"[11] and there must be such vigorous measures "as a warning to others"[12] without saying capital punishment was too severe. According to Origen, "They deserved to receive the penalty of the divine visitation in this world for the sin committed by the misappropriation."[13] Jerome was of like mind.[14]

The only voice we might consider contrary came from Basil of Caesarea, remarking that Ananias, "simultaneously with his wife, was given the death sentence and he was not deemed worthy to learn of any terms of penance for his sin nor did he even obtain an

7. Chrysostom, "Homily 8," *Paul the Apostle to Thessalonians* (*NPNF* 1 13:359).

8. Chrysostom, "Homily 18," *Acts of the Apostles* (*NPNF* 1 11:115).

9. Chrysostom, "Homily 12," *Acts of the Apostles* (*NPNF* 1 11:77).

10. *Contra Novatianum*, in Ambrosiaster, *Questions on Old and New*, 310. *Contra Novatianum* is an anonymous Latin work from sometime after the middle of the third century CE. It appears in Pseudo-Augustini Quaestiones Veteris et Novi Testamenti CXXVII as at one time having been ascribed to Augustine of Hippo. It is not the same as the anonymous *Ad Novatianum* (*ANF* 5:657–63), which was composed a few years after Cyprian's ministry.

11. Chrysostom, *Commentary on the Psalms*, Ps 6, 1:99.

12. Chrysostom, "Homily 18," *Acts of the Apostles* (*NPNF* 1 11:115).

13. Origen, *Gospel of St. Matthew* 15.15 (Heine, 1:205–6).

14. Jerome, "Letter 130.14 to Demetrias," *Letters of Saint Jerome* (*NPNF* 2 6:268).

opportunity for remorse nor time to do penance."[15] On the other hand, Chrysostom replied that by asking Sapphira the same question as he had asked Ananias about the price, Peter was giving her an opportunity to show remorse or repentance and to formulate a confession of wrongdoing, or a defense, or to ask for forgiveness.[16]

Jerome summarized the situation:

> There is no cruelty in regard for God's honour. Wherefore also in the Law it is said: "If thy brother or thy friend or the wife of thy bosom entice thee from the truth, thine hand shall be upon them and thou shalt shed their blood, and so shalt thou put the evil away from the midst of Israel."[17]

In any event, Acts 5:5–10 provide a prelude to the early Christian mindset toward the rigors in forgiving sin after baptism, and why penitents acquiesced to them.

RESEARCH QUESTION AND THESIS STATEMENT

This thesis examines the following question: Was the forgiveness of sins committed after Christian baptism a matter of local regulation between a major development in the mid-third century until another major change in 391 CE? This thesis shows the churches' practices for the forgiveness of postbaptismal sins were largely governed by local or congregational authorities rather than a central body over the whole church in the Roman Empire or world at large.

MOTIVATION

The motivation behind this thesis is to find an escape from the interpretation of the New Testament that reconciliation with God for sin after baptism is unlikely, or obtainable only by onerous

15. Basil, *Preface on the Judgment* 50.

16. Chrysostom, *Beginning of Acts* 3.5.

17. Jerome, "Letter 109.3 to Riparius," *Letters of Saint Jerome* (*NPNF* 2 6:213).

works of uncertain efficacy. To me, pre-Decian sources contain a distinction between two ways of salvation: one for non-Christians coming to Christ for the first time (conversion) and another for Christians who had sinned after conversion, for which rigorous acts are necessary to maintain or recapture it.

The thesis provides more historical details and analysis than the *Catechism of the Catholic Church* (1997) and points to a fundamental consensus that such forgiveness was solely within the jurisdiction of local bishops, not the pope or a churchwide legislator, such as the papal curia or ecumenical council.

LITERATURE REVIEW

I did not find a full exposition on my precise topic. The nearest to an exception is an article that cites my own previous work.[18] Its author concentrates on theory and theology while my work is on the practices, institutions, mechanics, and authority for forgiving postbaptismal sin. He traces anomalies in practice to inconsistencies among the apostles themselves, while I conclude that they are due to the jurisdiction of each local bishop, which are not necessarily incompatible.

The secondary authors fail to elaborate if, how, and by whom forgiving postbaptismal sins was a congregational option, while some assume the ultimate authority was regional, most notably in western Europe and northwest Africa on the one hand and in Anatolia on the other.[19] ("Anatolia" is sometimes known today as Asiatic Turkey or Asia Minor.) The exception to their general rule was the Council of Elvira in Spain, whose decrees resemble the East rather than the West.[20] Little or no space is given to Alexandria (northeastern Africa) or the influential church of Antioch, but my own research uncovered almost nothing for them. There is a similar paucity of ancient material favoring the Novatianist

18. Mokhoathi, "Christian Piety and Pardon."

19. Poschmann, *Penance*; Rahner, *Penance*.

20. Council of Elvira, *Canons*.

position, which I think was probably destroyed by the mainline church after the controversy.

The earlier twentieth century was dominated by Anglican authors, usually ones who advocated the revival of the stricter rules of the ancient church.[21] Two Roman Catholic scholars filled the void of the later twentieth century but resorted to speculation in order to demonstrate that present-day Roman Catholic practices can be inferred from the early sources. Rahner in particular relies too much on recent authors and spends too much time on various theologies, to the detriment of history proper or the ancient practice(s) that are the subject of my thesis.[22] The other Roman author was Bernhard Poschmann.[23] His coverage is from the New Testament to the Council of Trent. I am reluctant to put much reliance on him because he makes pro-Roman Catholic assumptions similar to Karl Rahner's selective presentism.

J. Patout Burns's *Cyprian the Bishop* outlines the forces and church factions that influenced Cyprian and the Carthage and Roman churches in the evolution of forgiveness of postbaptismal sins.[24] Burns offers comprehensive treatment of the motives and claims of martyrs and Cyprian's other opponents, seldom dealt with at length in other secondary sources.

Allan D. Fitzgerald's entry on "Penance" in *The Oxford Handbook of Early Christian Studies* states in a nutshell what my research has revealed from translations of original sources:

> Jesus did not leave an unambiguous set of instructions for Christian penance. Local churches had to appropriate scriptural directives within their own context. Hence, unity of practice—in rite and in law—was a result of historical development, not a point of departure.[25]

21. Haslehurst, *Penitential Discipline*; Mortimer, *Origins of Private Penance*; Watkins, *History of Penance*.

22. Rahner, *Penance*.

23. Poschmann, *Penance*.

24. Burns, *Cyprian*.

25. Fitzgerald, "Penance," 789.

This succinctly accounts for all the contradictions and chaos in the study of the ancient practices.

Some modern authors treat only one geographic area, a treatment that does not give a full view of how forgiveness had operated, or assert that the local bishop or congregation was the ultimate authority, rather than regional councils.[26] None of the sources isolate the local option as the chief institution for forgiveness of postbaptismal sins, the original observation of the thesis.

LOCATION OF AND NEED FOR RESEARCH

My sources fit into the field by capitalizing on today's unprecedented access to ancient church writings, both because some of them were not yet discovered until our time and because they are available on the internet. My research contributes to scholarly knowledge in the history of penance and absolution for sin for general histories of the subject, which is of special value in seminaries and theological departments. The thesis will update the available knowledge of forgiveness from the early twentieth century, when the last monographs from a Protestant viewpoint were published, and serve as a check on the claims in Roman Catholic ones.

SCOPE AND LIMITATIONS

My research will cover the possibility and procedures for forgiving postbaptismal sin from the Decian Persecution and mass apostasy in 249 to 251 CE until the beginning of the abolition of the office of "priest penitentiary" in 391 CE. The earlier date was marked by a major revolution in the scope and practice of pardoning and the establishment of priests penitentiary to hear and absolve from all sins in a parish or diocese. The sources of research result from efforts to include all writings that I could find by Christians in the Roman Empire from the middle of the third century to the end of

26. Halliburton, "Godly Discipline"; Mortimer, *Origins of Private Penance*; Silvas, *Basil of Caesarea*; Slusser, *Life and Works*.

the fourth. I hope these sources will show that my previous conclusions on the subject[27] were erroneous or overcome by the later development of Christianity, yet still close to the beginning of both Christianity and the authors in my book on the subject.

The research covers all writings originally written in this time period that I could find by and about early Christians from the period of study currently available to me in published English, French translations, or through Google Translate. It does not use sources in their original languages. It also does not include writings from those outside the Roman Empire or writings by women or other marginalized groups who did not write or whose material has been lost or not available in English or French. The research covers writings by Augustine prior to his ordination as presbyter in 391 CE, but not afterwards.

Running throughout the thesis is the role of local bishops in the reconciliation process. The only conclusion from differences among churches, inter-congregational deliberations, the gross contradictions in who is eligible for pardon, the wide differences in what the backsliders must do to obtain forgiveness and the limitations on them, as well as ancient original statements, is that all aspects of the penitential process were under the control of the local bishop in each parish or diocese, with no policy or enforcement by a supervisory or policy body covering the whole Christian religion, either universally or in the Roman Empire.

METHODOLOGY

I consulted all the contemporaneous writings by Christians in the Roman Empire from the middle of the third century to the end of the fourth that I could find available to me in English, French, or Google Translate and tried to produce a consensus of all authors. If there was no consensus among the ancients, I gave both (or all) sides and tried to find a common theme accounting for the differences. For writings in *The Ante-Nicene Fathers: Translations*

27. Brattston, "Forgiveness of Post-Baptismal Sin"; Brattston, *Can Sins Be Forgiven?*

of the Writings of the Fathers down to A.D. 325 and *Nicene and Post-Nicene Fathers*, I selected only material the indexes indicated as relevant to the thesis. I also read relevant material I found on Novanet, the American Theological Library Association (ATLA) Religion Database, and Google Scholar. I did not look at the works Biblindex did not indicate as citing the relevant New Testament authorities.

The scholarly paradigm is historical, roughly in chronological order, but divided by different geographic and cultural areas. The thesis concentrates on ancient actual practice and where practice is inextricably linked with doctrine.

My historical approach hopes to refute my previous publications that the New Testament distinguishes between two ways of salvation: an easy one for non-Christians coming to Christ for the first time (conversion) through faith alone—or faith, repentance, and baptism—with another for Christians who sinned after conversion entailing rigorous acts of uncertain efficacy.

I took into consideration all accessible authors, each in his or her own time period, regardless of whether they were considered orthodox by their own or a later age. I let all voices accessible to me be heard.

WORKING OUTLINE

Chapter 1 introduces the persistence of sin in the Christian church in the first few centuries from its beginnings and the questions studied in the thesis; whether it believed there is pardon for any sins committed after water baptism, whether it treated all sins as remissible after baptism, or whether there were exceptions, and who on earth could grant remission of them. The chapter specializes on the process and grounds for forgiving postbaptismal sins before the Decian Persecution of 249 to 251 CE and touches on the role of the bishop in the process. It also gives background and problems in the period between the New Testament and the Decian Persecution, ending where the substance of the thesis begins. It presents the embryo of later institutions of pardon, with each congregation, or each diocese, or its bishop holding a vaguely defined role, and posits that the roles were fleshed out after the Persecution, with the bishop still holding a central place.

Chapter 2 begins with a case study of Bishop Cyprian of Carthage to illustrate the sudden revolution in clerical thought and procedure about forgiveness of postbaptismal sins. It examines the writings and practice of contemporaries in both the western and eastern Mediterranean church and of Christians who resisted the development for dealing with repentant sinners, most significantly, repentant apostates. Part of the changes was the institution of the office of the priest penitentiary, a presbyter or deacon who specialized in hearing confessions of sins, prescribing penances, and forgiving penitent backsliders in heaven and on earth. The chapter also touches on the method and means of forgiveness in the era. The sins covered and pardoning process indicate that although overseas congregations were consulted, all voices thought forgiveness was a local matter and to be administered by local bishops or their delegates.

Chapter 3 highlights and describes that the situations in chapter 2 were not unanimous but entailed dissent and other approaches to the decisions recorded there, thus emphasizing that each bishop proceeded independently. This chapter details the opposition voices, the important matter of minor or venial sins, and the unforgivable sin or sin unto death.

Chapter 4 deals with the mechanics of forgiveness, including differences in prescribed actions and behaviors constituting penances and frameworks in the West, Anatolia, Egypt, and Antioch with Syria. The different penitential procedures in different geographic regions indicate that individual bishops or their delegates were in charge of the procedure. The time lengths of the penitential periods differed from a few weeks to several years, depending on the part of the Roman Empire, and probably from local bishop to local bishop. The thesis surveys the history of inter-congregational and inter-diocesan councils to conclude that such bodies exercised no influence on the local bishops, either in substance or in discretion. This chapter thus contributes to the thesis by demonstrating the local bishops' central role and their jurisdiction to prescribe the process, without referring to a churchwide or empire-wide mechanism.

The conclusion answers the question of whether there was a difference between the forgiveness of prebaptismal and postbaptismal sins, with the latter being much harder to obtain than the former. It details all aspects of the process and its administrators after the Cyprianic revolution. Some authors assumed that lesser penances were appropriate for venial sins, such as simple prayer, fasting, and almsgiving. The thesis notes the difference in these aspects from region to region, as instituted by local bishops. The conclusion of the thesis is that administrative procedures and contents were always local, with no supervisory or regulatory hierarchy.

1

Statement of the Problem and Background

THIS CHAPTER INTRODUCES THE questions studied in the thesis:

- whether the early church (250–391 CE) believed there is pardon for any sins committed after water baptism;
- whether the early church believed all sins are remissible after baptism, or are there exceptions;
- what actions the early church believed constituted an appropriate manifestation of sorrow and remorse for sins committed after baptism; and
- which officers of the early church held authority to hear and adjudicate confessions of sins committed after baptism and declare them forgiven on earth and in heaven.

The thesis answers the above questions as disclosed around the period of the "priests-penitentiary," between 250 and 391 CE. This chapter also gives background and problems in the period between the New Testament and the Decian Persecution, ending where the substance of the thesis begins.

INTRODUCTION

In 1991, I published an article that examined whether and how sins committed after Christian baptism could be forgiven.[1] It surveyed all primary sources from the period then available to me by and about Christians written prior to the devastating epidemic, mass apostasy, and thoroughgoing persecution under Emperor Decius in the middle of the third century CE. The article drew a number of dismal conclusions about the eternal fate of Christians who had sinned after baptism. It accepted Heb 6:4–6 and 10:26–31, which are quoted later in this thesis, and other early writings in their literal sense, all the while hoping I might find some equivalent early Christian authority to obtain a less depressing interpretation. Finding none, I concluded that any reconciliation with God for sin after baptism was unlikely, or obtainable only by onerous works of uncertain efficacy. I have since realized that I ought to have dealt critically with the sources, instead of giving them equal weight and authority. In the meantime, publishing additional books and articles synthesizing ancient and contemporary Christianity has improved my grasp of the field, materially increased by my studies at Acadia Divinity College.

My difficulty lay in the distinction between pre- and postbaptismal sins. The New Testament offers of forgiveness through faith alone (or faith, repentance, and baptism) appeared to me to have been addressed only to unconverted Jews and pagans, without more effort or input by the individual, such as loving obedience or works-righteousness. To me, the New Testament and other pre-Decian sources contained a distinction between two ways of salvation: one for non-Christians coming to Christ for the first time (conversion) and another for Christians who had sinned after conversion, for which rigorous acts are necessary to maintain or recapture it. This is in accord with the treatment of the latter in Heb 6:4–6 and 10:26–31. I recognize that few or no New Testament scholars agree with this view. To my knowledge, neither does any

1. Brattston, "Forgiveness of Post-Baptismal Sin," later expanded into the book *Can Sins Be Forgiven After Baptism?*

organized denomination, although in the time scope of this thesis, there were two major groups that accepted it: the Montanists and the Novatianists, of which more follows.

According to leading Anglican writer Gerald Bray, "It was believed by many Christians in the early church period that sins were taken away in baptism, and that if a baptized person sinned again, he or she would lose his or her salvation, because there was no further remedy for the offense committed."[2]

My assessment of the difference was confirmed by Christopher D. Marshall, who writes that references to repentance are common in the Lukan Acts, New Testament letters, and the Revelation of John. In them, repentance has two main meanings. The first is the convert's initial response to and acceptance of the gospel, entailing water baptism and membership in the church. This may be called "conversion" and marks a complete reorientation of the convert's life and commitment to Christian teaching (Acts 17:30; Rom 2:4–5; 2 Pet 3:9). The new believer was committed to lifelong practice of Christian teaching, a life of holiness, and desistance from sin (2 Cor 7:9–10, 12:21; Gal 6:1–2; 1 John 1:8–9; see also, Luke 17:3–4). But what if the Christian committed sins after baptism? This is where the second meaning comes in. In the second meaning, such postbaptismal repentance is often called "penitence." It involved a second repentance and recommitment to a holy life.

> Conversion and penitence have similar features, but the early church apparently saw something qualitatively distinctive about initial repentance. This is evident, for example, in the ambivalence in the New Testament over the standing of believers who had renounced their initial conversion, then subsequently relented and sought readmission to the community.[3]

Churchmen differed among themselves as to whether penitence could have the same effect as conversion; some thought that repentance from a sin committed after baptism was of no avail and

2. Bray, *Anglicanism*, 64.

3. Marshall, "Repentance," *Oxford Encyclopedia of the Bible*.

the backslider was lost forever, no matter how repentant he or she was (Heb 6:1–6; see also, 3:12), while other church writers thought a second forgiveness to be feasible (Jas 5:19–20), although burdensome and unlikely (2 Pet 2:20–22).[4]

At least I was not alone in my dismal exegesis or in distinguishing postbaptismal sins from prebaptismal.

After months of research and comparison, I concluded that there was no uniform Christian procedure for forgiving at least some sins, but rather everything depended on the local congregation's bishop or parish council,[5] a conclusion that this thesis will demonstrate was obtained in the years between 249 and 391. It will also show that the possibility of pardon for some sins but not others was not the same for all authors but varied from New Testament times onwards. The ancient church through many lands was unanimous in leaving forgiveness to a local option.

SIN WAS COMMON AFTER BAPTISM

The earliest successors of Christ and the apostles sinned so much after conversion and water baptism that the church provided standard routines for reconciling baptized sinners to God and the church. Written for a Christian readership, the first chapter of 1 John clearly states in verse 8, "If we say that we have no sin, we deceive ourselves, and the truth is not in us," and 10, "If we say that we have not sinned, we make him a liar, and his word is not in us." Verses 2:9 and 2:11 are to a like effect. In writing to the Christians at Corinth, the apostle Paul exhorted, "Be reconciled to God" (2 Cor 5:20), which would indicate that there was a reconciliation further to that in baptism or conversion. The apostle would have encouraged Christians to reconcile with God only if they had somehow lost their original reconciliation, and a further peacemaking was possible. This situation necessarily assumes both

4. Marshall, "Repentance."

5. Socrates Scholasticus, *Ecclesiastical History* 4.28.

postbaptismal sin and a means of being forgiven from it, a proposition related in subsequent literature.

Postbaptismal sinning was so widespread and frequent that Origen could preach about "those of us who sin daily and who perhaps do not spend a day of our life without sin."[6] His *Homilies on Ezekiel* 12.1.3 and *Homilies on Joshua* 5.6 assume that Christians have sinned after baptism. He categorized himself and others as postbaptismal sinners[7] and mentions that such sin was common among presbyters and deacons.[8] At one point, he adverts to "serious sins (the kind that most of the laity commit)."[9] Before him, Tertullian wrote of sins of daily committal, to which we all are liable: "For who will be free from the accident of either being angry unjustly, and retaining his anger beyond sunset; or else even using manual violence or else carelessly speaking evil; or else rashly swearing; or else forfeiting his plighted word or else lying."[10] Over a century later, Ambrose, in *On Repentance*, said, "What can show more pride than this, since the Scripture says: 'No one is free from sin, not even an infant of a day old' (Job 19.4),"[11] which is repeated in *Contra Novatianum*.[12] Lactantius's *Divine Institutes* 6.13 held only deliberate sins, not due to weakness, were irremissible.

Likewise, near the close of our period of study, John Chrysostom mentioned repeated sin after water baptism,[13] and Theodore of Mopsuestia noted, "It is impossible to be so completely free from sin as to have no need of confession at all."[14]

In short, all early writers who commented on the subject taught that Christians still continued to sin after their baptisms,

6. Origen, *Numbers* 8.1.5 (Scheck, 33).
7. Origen, *Jeremiah* 20.8.2–3; Origen, *Joshua* 1.7.
8. Origen, *Jeremiah* 12.3.1.
9. Origen, "Commentariorum 49," in *Gospel of St. Matthew* (Heine, 2:624).
10. Tertullian, *On Modesty* 19 (*ANF* 4:97).
11. Ambrose, *Repentance* 1.1.4 (*NPNF* 2 10:329).
12. *Contra Novatianum*, in Ambrosiaster, *Questions on Old and New*.
13. Chrysostom, *Concerning the Statues* 12.1.
14. Theodore, *Commentary on Psalms 1–81*, 5 Ps 38 (Hill, 439).

and hence, they needed to repent from and confess them, although not all such sins were serious but could be cleansed with little ado.

HOW SOME POSTBAPTISMAL SINS WERE FORGIVEN BEFORE THE DECIAN PERSECUTION

Tertullian's *On Modesty* 2 suggests that the Catholic church and the Montanists both regarded some sins to be forgivable and others unforgivable, but the rest of the treatise renders it unclear whether this was the firm position of either group.

If some sins are forgivable after baptism, there arises the question as to how many times a Christian can be redeemed from them. Is only one restoration allowed? Can all sins be forgiven again with the same effect as in baptism? May a Christian sin and be restored, sin and be restored, again and again, his or her whole spiritual life?

On one side of the issue is the *Shepherd of Hermas*, dating from the first half of the second century, in which the thesis is clearly set out: "There is but one repentance to the servants of God."[15] The penultimate paragraph of *Didascalia* 10 provides, "When he is gone forth twice from the Church, he is justly cut off,"[16] but it does not elaborate.

From Tertullian *On Modesty* 2, it would appear that both the Montanists and the Catholics divided sins into two categories:

> Some will be remissible, some irremissible: in accordance wherewith it will be doubtful to no one that some deserve chastisement, some condemnation. Every sin is dischargeable either by pardon or else by penalty: by pardon as the result of chastisement, by penalty as the result of condemnation.[17]

Another interpretation is this:

15. *Hermas*, mandate 4.1.8 (*ANF* 2:21).
16. *Didascalia* 10 (Connolly, 108).
17. Tertullian, *Modesty* 2 (*ANF* 4:76); see also Joyce, "Private Penance," 26.

> We think that it should be evident to anyone who considers this passage with due care, that Tertullian is here speaking of sins for which public penance would not be imposed. Public penance with its attendant humiliations as described in the *De Paenitentia*, presupposed that the sinner was spiritually dead: that the Holy Spirit no longer dwelt in his soul: that he needed to recover once again the life bestowed upon him in Baptism.[18]

Origen was of like mind:

> Some mortal fault finds us which does not consist in a mortal offense, not in a blasphemy of the faith . . . but consists in a vice of words or habits . . . this kind of fault can always be repaired, and it is never forbidden for you to do penance for offenses of this kind. For in more serious offenses, a place is given only once for penance; but these common ones which we frequently commit, always receive repentance and are bought back without interruption.[19]

Such variations illustrate that Christians' jurisdiction to forgive entailed a wide latitude everywhere, and their bishops exercised it in different contexts and to different extents, with attempts by church councils to give guidelines within their local region. Of course, there could have been abuse of discretion and misapprehension as to how far it reached and to which sins they pertained.[20] Cyprian indicated that bishops possessed such discretion and that the kinds of sins that some would consider remissible varied from place to place, even in pre-Decian times:

> Among our predecessors, some of the bishops here in our province thought that peace was not to be granted to adulterers, and wholly closed the gate of repentance against adultery. Still they did not withdraw from the assembly of their co-bishops, nor break the unity of the Catholic Church by the persistency of their severity or censure; so that, because by some peace was granted to

18. Joyce, "Private Penance," 28.

19. Origen, *Leviticus* 15.2.6 (Barkley, 258).

20. Origen, *On Prayer* 18.

> adulterers, he who did not grant it should be separated from the Church. While the bond of concord remains, and the undivided sacrament of the Catholic Church endures, every bishop disposes and directs his own acts, and will have to give an account of his purposes to the Lord.[21]

Origen's *Leviticus* 2.4.5 enunciated a compendium of procedures for entering or re-entering divine favor:

1. baptism for the remission of sins;
2. the suffering of martyrdom;
3. almsgiving;
4. forgiving the sins of your brothers;
5. converting a sinner from the error of his way: "He which converteth the sinner from the error of his way shall save a soul from death, and shall hide a multitude of sins" (Jas 5:20 KJV);
6. an abundance of love: Christ himself said, "Her sins, which are many, are forgiven; for she loved much" (Luke 7:47 KJV) and Simon Peter said, "[love] covers a multitude of sins" (1 Pet 4:8);[22] and
7. penances (paenitentia), being voluntary spiritual and physical afflictions of various severity and rigor, sometimes called "exomologesis."

An eighth was added by Theodore of Mopsuestia, as disclosed later in this thesis.

As for baptism for the remission of sins, the early sources following are clear that a person can be baptized only once, although some likened penance to "a second baptism."

21. Cyprian, *Letters* (*ANF* 5:332).

22. Origen, *Leviticus* 2.4.5 (Barkley, 47).

Martyrdom

The greatest relevance of martyrdom was that intending martyrs, termed "confessors," could assign the benefits of their suffering and death to remit the sins of repentant backsliders. Such vicarious sacrifice was common during the Decian Persecution, at least at Carthage[23] and Alexandria,[24] but the church abolished it as a means of salvation shortly afterwards, because of abuses, such as a martyr signing a blank document of forgiveness, for the names of backsliders to be added later, without limit on the number.[25]

A few years before the Decian Persecution, Origen was apprehensive because there were then few or no martyrdoms to take away sins, the previous forty years having been free of government persecutions against Christian laity.[26]

Repentance

The most common method for forgiveness of sins, both before and after Decius, was an institution or discipline called "repentance." It entailed more than remembering your misdeed(s), silently asking God for pardon, and quietly resolving to change your life. The ancient system of forgiveness was more similar to the modern Roman Catholic institution of performing certain prescribed spiritual exercises, often outward ones, but was much more extensive and harsh.

As the local dispenser of pardon, the local bishop needed to first determine whether the backslider was truly repentant.[27] Limiting it to only one occasion in a lifetime, Hermas said such repentance must be with your whole heart and "he who repents

23. Tertullian, *To the Martyrs* 1; Tertullian, *On Modesty* 22; Cyprian, *Letters* 15, 26, 27.

24. Dionysius, "Letter to Fabius," in Eusebius Caesarea, *Church History* 6.42.5–6.

25. Cyprian, *Letters* 15.4, 27.1.

26. Origen, *Numbers* 10.2.1–2.

27. *Didascalia* 6.

must torture his own soul, and be exceedingly humble in all his conduct, and be afflicted with many kinds of affliction."[28] First Clement 48.1 exhorted, "Let us fall down before the Lord, and beseech Him with tears, that He would mercifully be reconciled to us."[29] Justin indicated that restoration was given to backsliders who wept, mourned, and repented.[30] Origen exhorted backsliders in his congregation to repent, pray, and fast over their sins,[31] and confess and lament them.[32] He preached that such repentance must be vigorously pursued and involve an inflamed soul, a heart pricked and in torment, and mastering oneself so as not to commit the sin again.[33] The repentant backslider punishes his conscience, tortures his heart, is unable to eat or drink, and fasts out of grief and repentance, "not only for one day nor one night but for a long time."[34] These practices continued into the post-Decian era, including under the priests penitentiary, who are discussed later in this thesis.

Tertullian wrote that repentance was necessary both in proto-orthodoxy[35] and in Montanism.[36] Origen's *Homilies on Numbers* specified, "Be converted to repentance without pretense, to bewail our past, to be on guard for the future, to invoke God's help; for immediately when you convert and groan, you will be saved."[37] In *Commentary on the Gospel of John* 20.12,[38] he mentioned repentance as the beginning of restoring oneself after a postbaptismal sin. Putting repentance in perspective, he preached that it is not through bodily punishments or penances that sins are taken away

28. *Hermas* similitude 3.7 (*ANF* 2:38).
29. 1 Clem. 48.1 (*ANF* 1:18).
30. Justin Martyr, *Dialogue* 141.
31. Origen, *Joshua* 1.7, 5.6.
32. Origen, *1 Corinthians* 24.
33. Origen, *Psalm 37* 1.1.
34. Origen, *Jeremiah* 20.9.1 (Smith, 240).
35. Tertullian, *Repentance* 9.
36. Tertullian, *Modesty* 19.
37. Origen, *Numbers* 8.1.9 (Scheck, 35).
38. Heine, 89–90.

but through repentance.[39] He also noted that sins after baptism are washed away by tears of repentance. Later churchmen detailed the activities through which repentance is to be manifested. Apparently, it was the sinner's local bishop who decided whether the remorse and penance were enough in particular cases.

My book concluded that based on such early church sources, readers who had sinned after baptism should enter upon

> thorough, intense, and heartfelt repentance—even fasting, if it helps—as a means of reconciliation, proceeding from "a sound, genuine and holy faith,"[40] the sort that leads to almsgiving, forgiving the sins of your siblings, converting a sinner from the error of his ways, and abundant love.[41]

However, I wrote this without full knowledge of what repentance consisted of, due to lack of elaborations in the pre-Decian sources.

According to one fairly early twentieth-century summation, "Ignatius of Antioch, Dionysius of Corinth, Clement of Alexandria, all speak of the pardon accorded by the Church to penitent sinners, and no one of them hints that there were sins which the Church could not, or would not, remit."[42] However, this statement is too general and does not distinguish between prebaptismal and postbaptismal trespasses; but this may indicate only that the author believed there was no such distinction.

As mentioned above, the earliest successors of Christ and the apostles sinned so much after water baptism that the church provided standard routines for reconciling penitent backsliders. Nobody before the middle of the third century CE was sure whether these routines would, in effect, counterbalance major sins or which sins could be forgiven on earth. Montanists and Novatianists denied they could. The clear answer came during a revolution in church thinking after 249 CE, which is the topic of my next chapter.

39. Origen, *Leviticus* 11.2.6 (Barkley, 214).

40. Origen, *Leviticus* 3.8.7 (Barkley, 69).

41. Brattston, *Can Sins Be Forgiven*, 93.

42. Joyce, "Private Penance," 24.

2

Forgiveness Found: The Cyprianic Revolution

CYPRIAN: A CASE STUDY

THIS CHAPTER DETAILS A major readjustment as to how the church could forgive postbaptismal sins, with much of the western church beginning to hold the sentiments of Cyprian, the bishop of Carthage at the time. According to one leading scholar on the subject,

> The writings of St. Cyprian, and particularly his correspondence with the Roman Church, provide a graphic picture of the problems and controversies that arose at this time. Along with the testimony of Tertullian, they are the most important source for the history of penance up to the time of St. Augustine.[1]

This thesis ends the year Augustine was ordained presbyter.

In 247 CE, Thascius Caecilius Cyprianus (martyred 258) was elected bishop by the laity and clergy of the Christian community in Carthage, in what is Tunisia today. The Decian Persecution

1. Poschmann, *Penance*, 53.

began two years later, causing a mass apostasy of Christians in the Roman Empire through Christians sacrificing to pagan gods in worship in accordance with imperial decree.

By centering on the situation of one churchman, this chapter outlines the sorts of options and influences a pardoner (usually a local bishop) needed to choose from, which in turn discloses that the decisions were not hastily or lightly made. Cyprian shopped around, as it were, for second opinions from other bishops, at least one over a thousand kilometers away. In his correspondence, he does not threaten anyone outside his diocese if they do not copy his policies. The evidence lacks references to any central body over more than one bishopric or any pressure other than polite interchanges in written correspondence. Inter-congregational or inter-diocesan councils enacting compulsory rules may only have been coming into existence and did not yet exercise the authority they held under the reign of Constantine, if indeed they did not originate first in his time. The evidence favors the later period.[2]

At first, before the end of the persecution, Cyprian opined in *On the Dress of Virgins* 2, "There is no further pardon for sinning after you have begun to know God."[3] Cyprian fled into hiding during the Decian Persecution. Some of his letters from there[4] show the evolution of his thought. He advanced the idea that in order to obtain forgiveness of postbaptismal sins, it is not enough that a penitent rely on the complete satisfaction by Christ but must make his/her own atonement and satisfaction for his/her sins. According to him and contemporary Christian teachers, pardon for postbaptismal sin can be obtained only with severe difficulty, with long, hard requirements for forgiveness.[5] "Cyprian seems to have assumed from the beginning that the sin of idolatry could be forgiven, at least by Christ, perhaps through the intercession of the martyrs, and that the penitent lapsed could be reconciled

2. Brattston, *Rise of Bishops*, 24–28.

3. Cyprian, *Dress of Virgins* 2 (*ANF* 5:430–31).

4. Cyprian, *Letters* 12, 13, 15, 16, 23–24, 33–36, 42; Cyprian, *Letter* 30 "Roman Clergy to Cyprian."

5. Cyprian, *On the Lapsed* 3.

to the church."[6] The most common mode of idolatry at the time was apostasy to the Roman gods by sacrificing to them according to the imperial decree. This was intended and regarded as a denial that Jesus is Lord and there is only one God. In dealing with it, Cyprian insisted on due penitential procedures and that there was hope of eventual forgiveness for apostates who performed them.

As previously mentioned, some Christians who chose death rather than apostatize gave letters to penitents conferring the sacrifice of their lives as a redemption of their sin. "Cyprian recognized the authority of the martyrs by allowing the presbyters to give peace to any dying penitents who held their letter of intercession."[7] Then, "once the Roman clergy had announced its policy of reconciling all the penitent lapsed at the time of death, however, Cyprian's position became untenable and he agreed to follow the common practice."[8] "Shortly thereafter, he extended this concession to all dying penitents, thus bringing his church's practice into line with that of the church in Rome where the confessors refused to issue such letters of peace."[9]

During Cyprian's ministry, forgiveness and restoration to the earthly church took place in stages and categories of sinners. The first class of repentant apostates to be forgiven were those who held letters of peace from martyrs, who were forgiven and allowed to receive communion on their deathbeds.[10] All other penitents had to wait until the various parts of the church arrived at a consensus of which and how other categories were to be forgiven. Cyprian ruled that no decision or action was to be taken until after the end of the Persecution, reasoning that the issue concerned all Christians and would require general consultation. Neither the confessors and martyrs, nor even the bishop, he explained, should presume to decide such a momentous and far-reaching question

6. Burns, *Cyprian*, 57.

7. Burns, *Cyprian*, 3.

8. Burns, *Cyprian*, 57.

9. Burns, *Cyprian*, 3.

10. Cyprian, *Letter* 18.1–2.

alone,[11] without "an assembly for counsel being gathered together, with bishops, presbyters, deacons, and confessors, as well as with the laity who stand fast,"[12] demonstrating that in this instance, practices were governed by local or congregational authorities.[13] Cyprian's decision to wait to hold this assembly was shared generally by influential people in the church.[14] It was opined that if "confessors chose to act unilaterally, admitting the lapsed to full communion by a personal and private judgment, they were robbing the Church of an opportunity to discern in common."[15]

Cyprian ended the practice of Christians about to be martyred writing documents recommending forgiveness, which some sorrowful apostates thought excused them from seeking absolution from the church or its clergy and from penitential exercises such as mourning, lamenting, weeping, etc.[16] Cyprian rebuked presbyters who granted absolution on no more than a recommendation by a martyr,[17] and such martyrs themselves.[18] He pointed out that while the Bible conferred the power to forgive on bishops as successors of the apostles, martyrs possessed no similar scriptural authority, "or even assurance of effective intercession" with God.[19]

However, the apostasy was in such unprecedented numbers and raised so many issues that Cyprian and the institutional church in the West perceived the wisdom in establishing a policy similar to those of other bishops, to give him more confidence that he was neither too lax nor too strict and to draw on their wisdom and experience, feeling doubts and lack of knowledge in himself to make the best possible decisions that were ultimately his. The

11. Burns, *Cyprian*, 248.

12. Cyprian, *Letter* 30.5 (*ANF* 5:310).

13. Cyprian, *Letter* 51.5 (*ANF* 5:334); see also, Burns, *Cyprian*, 80; Fitzgerald, "Model for Dialogue," 240, 249, 251, 253.

14. Burns, *Cyprian*, 81.

15. Fitzgerald, "Model for Dialogue," 248.

16. Cyprian, *Letters* 8.2, 15.1, 16, 24, 33.

17. Cyprian, *Letter* 17.2.

18. Cyprian, *Letter* 16.2; Burns, *Cyprian*, 81.

19. Burns, *Cyprian*, 86.

sheer extent and variety of his correspondence reveals that bishops of other places were similarly seeking to make good decisions. In particular, his correspondence with the church at Rome shows that they were reaching decisions by congregation or diocese, rather than anyone proposing a general council over any particular region of the Roman Empire. In an interim between bishops, the presbyters at Rome advised, "Remedies of a too hasty kind, and certainly not likely to avail, should be afforded for communion; and by a false mercy, new wounds should be impressed on the old wounds of their transgression; so that even repentance should be snatched from these."[20] Cyprian himself feared that if forgiveness was not extended to the apostates, they would give up hope and engage in greater sins, completely abandoning their Christian training and commitment, and that

> neither should hope of communion and peace be wholly denied to the lapsed, lest they should fail still more through desperation, and, because the Church was closed to them, should, like the world, live as heathens; nor yet, on the other hand, should the censure of the Gospel be relaxed, so that they might rashly rush to communion, but that repentance should be long protracted, and the paternal clemency be sorrowfully besought, and the cases, and the wishes, and the necessities of individuals be examined into.[21]

To hold such a council, the attendees would first need the freedom to travel openly, which meant it must be after the Persecution had ended.[22] Nor could it convene in the coming summer because hot weather brought diseases.[23] Not satisfied with this, Cyprian also corresponded with the church in the city of Rome to establish a wider consensus on the lapsed,[24] so that there would

20. Cyprian, *Letter* 30.3 "Roman Clergy to Cyprian" (*ANF* 5:309).

21. Cyprian, *Letter* 51.5 (ANF 5:328).

22. Cyprian, *Letter* 19.2, 23, 20.3, 55.4–6.

23. Cyprian, *Letter* 18.1.

24. Cyprian, *Letters* 27, 30, 35, 36; Cyprian and Second Council of Carthage, "Epistle to Cornelius" (*ANF* 53); Cyprian, *Letter* 30 "Roman Clergy to

be "no momentary nor over-hasty cure."[25] More than one such council was found necessary,[26] one of them because they feared another persecution was coming,[27] with the assumption that the church would soon need to work with even more apostates, and to strengthen the faithful against being forced to sacrifice.

Forgiveness was extended to apostates in stages and categories, with the scope of penitents expanding in steps over a few years. After penitents who had received certificates of absolution from persons in danger of martyrdom[28] came Christians who had been willing to sacrifice but were never called upon to do so.[29] An inter-congregational council at Carthage in 251 CE advised readmitting back into the church apostates who later reversed their action by approaching government authorities and offering to be martyred.[30] Next were those who did not actually sacrifice but had merely bribed government officials to issue false certificates that they had done so.[31]

The next category in time to be restored to the church, upon a review of their individual cases, were people who had actually sacrificed but had their property confiscated by the government and sometimes had been forced into exile[32] or had sacrificed only under threat and torture.[33] Soon, all applicants who exhibited remorse and reform were readmitted, even sacrificers, on their deathbeds if they performed penances until their deaths and were restored and communed in their last extremity.[34] The absolution

---

Cyprian."

25. Cyprian, *Letter* 30.6 "Roman Clergy to Cyprian" (*ANF* 5:310).

26. Cyprian, *Letters* 52.3, 55.6.

27. Cyprian, *Letter* 57.1.

28. Cyprian, *Letters* 18.1–2, 20.3.

29. Cyprian, *On the Lapsed* 28; Burns, *Cyprian*, 183–87.

30. Cyprian, *Letter* 24.

31. Burns, *Cyprian*, 86.

32. Cyprian, *Letters* 24–25.

33. Cyprian, *Letter* 55.13.

34. Cyprian, *Letter* 55.17.

remained even if the afflicted recovered and lived.[35] Finally, there was a general amnesty to everyone who exhibited signs of remorse, reformed themselves, and performed prescribed penitential exercises.[36] When the bishops met in spring 253 CE, the consensus recommended to bishops to admit all penitents to the Eucharist immediately, fearing a new outbreak of widespread persecution. They agreed on authorizing the admission of all the penitents into communion without further delay. The bishops argued that signs and warnings of a new outbreak of persecution had moved them to act. Penitent sacrificers no longer needed to wait until just before death.[37]

Although bishops were free from the higher authority that solidified under Constantine, the geographic reach and number of churchmen present at the African synod of 251 CE exerted a moral suasion rare for the time, such that it

> strengthened the position of each bishop in his own church. First, the individual bishops could appeal to the council's decision as a justification for the actions which they took or refused to take in their individual churches. Cyprian, for example, countered the Novatianist charge that he had changed his own rigorist position after the persecution by appealing to the decree of the council allowing the certified to be reconciled immediately and the sacrificers on their deathbeds.[38]

The decrees of the African and Roman councils gave no indication that apostasy had previously been considered unpardonable up to that time, nor do they mention the other most serious sins of fornication or murder, nor distinguish between forgivable and

35. Cyprian, *Letter* 55.13.

36. Cyprian, *Letter* 57.1, 3; Burns, *Cyprian*, 8, 62, 97–98, 157; Roitto, "Rituals of Reintegration," 430.

37. Burns, *Cyprian*, 8, 62, 97–98.

38. Burns, *Cyprian*, 87–88.

unforgivable.[39] Nowhere does Cyprian manifest that he thought pardoning apostasy was foreign to the apostolic tradition.[40]

As revealed by his correspondence, which shows Cyprian's indecision and groping for a solution as to how to reconcile a large host of repentant apostates, there was no established rule coming down from apostolic tradition, so the council of bishops needed to create a structure and procedure.[41] Nathaniel Marshall summarizes Cyprian's thought and actions:

> St. Cyprian was so clear in the case of those who had lapsed into idolatry during the rage of persecutions, that there can be no doubt of his opinion in that matter. And though we do not find him so express upon the two other crimes, yet from what hath been cited out of him, where he mentions the practice of some of his predecessors, with a note of their having differed from the usage of his own time, for that they did not allow of reconciliation to the sin of uncleanness [extramarital sex], I think we may fairly gather that it was his own usage to allow it. It is, moreover, certain that he looked upon faults which were not committed directly against God to be of a lower class, and of a less heinous nature, than others in which the honour of God was more immediately concerned. So did Gregory Nyssen after him. If, therefore, the more heinous were remitted, we may well conclude that the less heinous were not then esteemed irremissible.[42]

In short, Cyprian was inclined to forgiving sins of every nature and after due penances.

The various councils of Carthage and Rome, held within a period of three years in the 250s CE, opened the opportunity for penance and pardon for all sins, including apostasy, sexual immorality, and murder. As this thesis explains in a later chapter, the bishop possessed sole jurisdiction,[43] although he could de-

39. Quasten, *Patrology*, 2:380.

40. Quasten, *Patrology*, 2:381.

41. Marshall, *Penitential Discipline*, 89–90.

42. Marshall, *Penitential Discipline*, 89–90.

43. Cyprian, *Letters* 19.2, 55.4; Cyprian, *Letter* 30.8 "Roman Clergy to

pute a presbyter or deacon to exercise it.[44] There was nothing in Scripture or church tradition handed down from the apostles for him to violate. Indeed, he must have relied much on judgments of the officiating presbyter or deacon, collectively known as "priests penitentiary."

There were many factors and pressures in deciding what categories of sinners to forgive, such as laxists who would admit everyone,[45] rigorists who insisted on harsh penances but would nevertheless not forgive,[46] lapsed individuals themselves, and the threat of another persecution, which would produce more apostates, more Christians obtaining false certificates, more lapsed seeking forgiveness. In all these, according to Cyprian, penitents were to be treated on a case-by-case basis within the general categories set by the local "bishop, presbyters, deacons, and confessors, as well as with the laity who stand fast,"[47] and subject to the discretion of the local bishop.[48] Among these factors and pressures were the following:

1. Refusal to acknowledge penitents' commitment was unacceptable to many steadfast Christians and led to defections from the Catholic church. "Under pressure from both the faithful and the penitents, therefore, the bishops redrew the church's boundary to include the penitents and provide them the opportunity for salvation";[49]
2. On the other hand, too easy forgiveness would lead average Christians to believe apostasy and other sin a light matter and engage in it themselves, presuming pardon would be easily given. If faithful Christians see Communion given to

Cyprian."

44. Cyprian, *Letter* 18.1.
45. Cyprian, *Letter* 17.2.
46. E.g., Novatianists.
47. Cyprian, *Letter* 30.5 (*ANF* 5:310).
48. Cyprian, *Letter* 51.21.
49. Burns, *Cyprian*, 70.

a backslider who had not undergone penance, they may regard his/her misdeeds acceptable in the church's eyes and not sinful.[50]

3. "Too easy readmission of apostates makes a mockery of the martyrs who held firm in persecution."[51]
4. Although repentant, apostates were a threat to the church's integrity and very identity.

> Because they had polluted themselves by contact with the demonic rites of the imperial cult, they were a danger to the purity of the communion. Because they stood under the threat of repudiation by Christ for refusing to confess him on earth, their participation could destroy the eucharist as a symbol and foretaste of the heavenly banquet.[52]

5. God might punish communicants tainted by idolatry in apostasy by causing them to be burned by the consecrated bread or choked while drinking from the chalice.[53]
6. Tensions within the church lessened after the 251 CE reconciliation of Christians who had obtained false certificates of compliance and admission of the sacrificers as penitents—but rose again when peace was granted to penitents during the summer epidemic. "Some of the sacrificers admitted to communion on what were taken to be their deathbeds had then recovered and remained in communion while their fellows continued as penitents."[54]
7. Cyprian asserted that "the bishop is appointed by God for the governance of the church during the present time; judging belongs to him and submission to his authority is a necessary

50. Roitto, "Rituals of Reintegration," 437.
51. Roitto, "Rituals of Reintegration," 437.
52. Burns, *Cyprian*, 25.
53. Burns, *Cyprian*, 72.
54. Burns, *Cyprian*, 97.

sign of repentance."[55] Hence, the martyrs and laxist presbyters who granted easy forgiveness without penance were rebels against church (bishops') authority and ought to be curbed or dismissed.[56] When the bishops refused to approve their practice and maintained the decisions of local recent councils and their bishops, the laxists formed a rival ecclesiastical structure with its own bishops. The existence of this splinter group influenced Cyprian and his colleagues toward a more middle ground—or at least as a constant reminder that there was a more lenient force for the reconciliation of the lapsed.[57] Another rival denomination with its own college of bishops was the Novatianists, who denied that the church or anyone else could forgive on earth but nevertheless required lifelong austere penances in the uncertain hope that God might forgive in heaven.

In short, Cyprian did not introduce an entirely new policy for dealing with either lapsed laity or unworthy clergy. The custom of the Roman church and at least some parts of the African church had allowed penitents—even those who had accused themselves of apostasy—to be reconciled and readmitted to communion at the time of death. This position was announced by the presbyters of the church in Rome, and Cyprian himself adopted it under pressure from the community in Carthage even during the persecution.[58] Note that local bishops like Cyprian and the church at Rome were subject to various influences in the exercise of their discretion, as to what categories of backsliders to forgive, and what appeared to them as the details of good and appropriate penances.

Cyprian's summary reveals the great amount of thought, deliberation, and consultation with which Christians of the era proceeded, which would have been unnecessary if there was a general

55. Burns, *Cyprian*, 81.

56. Burns, *Cyprian*, 82.

57. Burns, *Cyprian*, 51.

58. Burns, *Cyprian*, 172.

authority over them, or the questions had been resolved by the apostles or other Christians in an earlier age.

ACTIONS THAT CONSTITUTE APPROPRIATE MANIFESTATION OF SORROW AND REMORSE FOR SINS

In the middle of the third century CE, a new feature appeared as a restoration process, or at least it is not found in earlier Christian documents, except "by thy hands thou shalt labour for the redemption of thy sins" in the *Epistle of Barnabas* 19.10.[59] Placed on top of the primitive mentions of heartfelt repentance, almsgiving, and forgiving and restoring other backsliders, there existed a system of bodily chastenings and mortification of the flesh. It appears to have taken literally Paul's instruction to "hand this man over to Satan for the destruction of the flesh, so that the spirit may be saved in the day of the Lord" (1 Cor 5:5), on which Origen noted that the procedure is not for the destruction of the soul nor the destruction of the spirit but for the destruction of the flesh. The flesh is destroyed so that the spirit is saved in the day of the Lord. Paul instructed that a particularly heinous backslider be expelled from the church in order to educate him, with the hope that he would repent and turn around (see Joel 2:14). The purpose is to destroy his engagement with the flesh, not to torment or derange him. Exclusion is in the hope that the sinner will confess and lament his sins, with fasting and weeping.[60]

With the debatable exception of weeping, sighing, and fasting in *Didascalia* 6, Tertullian was the first, and the only, church father before Decius to detail arduous and humiliating outward penances called "paenitentia" and "exomologesis." This system remained in force centuries afterwards and was one reason intending Christians delayed their baptisms until their deathbeds.[61] Moreover, some

59. *ANF* 1:148.

60. Origen, *First Corinthians* 24.

61. Bray, *Anglicanism*, 64.

church fathers believed that baptized persons who died outside a state of grace would receive more punishment in the afterlife than the unbaptized would.[62] Clement of Alexandria could not decide which was in the worse position.[63]

In this method of postbaptismal reconciliation, penitents would "sit in sackcloth and bristle in ashes; with the self-same weeping they groan; with the self-same prayers they make their circuits; with the self-same knees they supplicate."[64] Tertullian's *On Repentance* 9 indicated what the regime of physical penances required of the penitent:

> To lie in sackcloth and ashes, to cover his body in mourning, to lay his spirit low in sorrows, to exchange for severe treatment the sins which he has committed; moreover, to know no food and drink but such as is plain,—not for the stomach's sake, to wit, but the soul's; for the most part, however, to feed prayers on fastings, to groan, to weep and make outcries unto the Lord your God; to bow before the feet of the presbyters, and kneel to God's dear ones; to enjoin on all the brethren to be ambassadors to bear his deprecatory supplication.[65]

Tertullian's *On Repentance* 11 relates that penitents were "unwashen, sordidly attired, estranged from gladness, they must spend their time in the roughness of sackcloth, and the horridness of ashes, and the sunkenness of face caused by fasting."[66] This regime continued after Decius, with my fuller treatment below.

Eusebius gives an account of penance and restoration of a Christian who had been persecuted by the Roman government, became a bishop in a heresy, and sought to return to the mainline church during the episcopacy of Zephyrinus of Rome (AD 198 to 217):

62. Hippolytus, *Daniel* 1.25.4; Origen, *Jeremiah* 2.3.2; Origen, *Jeremiah* 16.7.1; Basil, *Christian Ethics* 11.2; Basil, *Letter* 22.

63. Clement, *Stromata* 2.13.

64. Tertullian, *On Modesty* 5 (*ANF* 4:78).

65. Tertullian, *Repentance* 11 (*ANF* 3:664).

66. Tertullian, *Repentance* 11 (*ANF* 3:665).

> He put on sackcloth and covered himself with ashes, and with great haste and tears he fell down before Zephyrinus, the bishop, rolling at the feet not only of the clergy, but also of the laity; and he moved with his tears the compassionate Church of the merciful Christ. And though he used much supplication, and showed the welts of the stripes which he had received, yet scarcely was he taken back into communion.[67]

A condition of forgiveness of postbaptismal sin was that the backslider undergo arduous and humiliating outward penances of various time lengths. Such condition had persisted from long before Cyprian and continued after him, although the specifics and lengths of time varied from time to time and place to place.

OTHER WESTERN EARLY CHURCH AUTHORS

The consensus of Cyprian and the bishops and congregations who agreed with him carried the day in the western Mediterranean and became permanent there. This section will show that, eventually, churches in the Roman Empire established venues for the forgiveness of even the most serious sins, with the process of forgiveness centered in the local bishop with specially commissioned presbyters and deacons to perform most of the work. This wide consensus is even more remarkable when we consider the autonomy and independent thinking of pre-Decian bishops as Cyprian described:

> And, indeed, among our predecessors, some of the bishops here in our province thought that peace was not to be granted to adulterers, and wholly closed the gate of repentance against adultery. Still they did not withdraw from the assembly of their co-bishops, nor break the unity of the Catholic Church by the persistency of their severity or censure; so that, because by some peace was granted to adulterers, he who did not grant it should be separated from the Church. While the bond of concord remains, and the undivided sacrament of the Catholic

67. Eusebius of Caesarea, *Church History* 5.28.12 (*NPNF* 2 10:248).

> Church endures, every bishop disposes and directs his own acts, and will have to give an account of his purposes to the Lord.[68]

Here, Cyprian cites pre-Decian practice to reveal that pardoning severe sins such as apostasy was not a novelty or departure from the tradition handed down from the apostles, and that local bishops exercised a great degree of independence in implementing and applying procedures.

Over a century after Cyprian, Ambrose of Milan interpreted Heb 6:4–6 in a manner amenable to forgiveness of postbaptismal offenses. Assuming Paul wrote this passage, he said it was to be explained through the apostle Paul's actions in his letters to the Corinthians in forgiving the man cohabiting with his father's wife. Paul had assigned a penance, or rather a cease-and-desist order, that the offender give up the relationship (1 Cor 5:1–5). When the sinner did so, Paul forgave him (2 Cor 2:5–10). Ambrose rhetorically asked, "Could Paul teach in opposition to his own act?" to show that the Hebrews passage is not to be applied literally in the full force of its words.[69] Ambrose accused the Novatianists of being inconsistent by forgiving sins they deemed minor while refusing to absolve ones they considered unforgivable on earth. He claimed this was inconsistent and contrary to the truth that the church can pardon all sins.[70]

Like the anonymous author of *Ad Novatianum*,[71] Ambrose did not distinguish between pre- and postbaptismal sins when quoting Scripture. Thus, he applied to backsliders all the promises in the New Testament that God will freely forgive sinners. The difference, he wrote, is that prebaptismal sins are cleansed in baptism and postbaptismal ones in penance. This flows from God having empowered his clergy to forgive sins, either through baptism or through penance.[72]

68. Cyprian, *Letter* 51.21 (*ANF* 5:332).

69. Ambrose, *Repentance* 2.2.6–7 (*NPNF* 2 10:345).

70. Ambrose, *Repentance* 1.3.11.

71. *Treatise Against the Heretic Novatian* (*ANF* 5:657–63).

72. Ambrose, *Repentance* 1.2.7, 1.3.10–11, 1.8.36, 2.2.12.

Bishop Pacian of Barcelona, who lived at the same time as Ambrose in the middle of the fourth century, accepted the redemptive regime of Cyprian largely because of "acceptance of reconciliations by Cyprian, Cornelius and other martyrs"[73] and their respective characters as against those of Novatianists. Pacian did not cite a higher church authority covering all congregations. The name of Cyprian of Carthage was still held in high esteem in the western Mediterranean.[74] Pacian added a reason of his own in two different works: "The Apocalypse also threatens the seven Churches unless they should repent. Nor would he, indeed, threaten the impenitent unless he pardoned the penitent,"[75] and, "Never would God threaten the unrepentant unless he would pardon the penitent."[76]

Reflecting the general position of the mainstream western church, *Contra Novatianum* addresses the question from another viewpoint:

> What idea would we have of God, if he had mercy on his enemies without demanding penance, and refused it to his repentant friends? . . . He would have looked for an opportunity to lose men rather than save them. But far from us this thought, for Our Lord said: "The Son of man did not come to lose souls, but to save them." (Luke 9:56) If God makes it our duty to forgive us up to seventy times seven times the sins we commit against each other, on the sole condition that we repent (Matt. 18:22), how much more will he forgive those who have offended him and come back to him? God wants the conversion of every sinner.[77]

73. Pacian, *Letter* 3 (Hanson, 44–45).

74. Pacian, *Letters* 1–3 (Hanson 28–29, 35, 44, 64–65).

75. Pacian, *On Penitents* 12(3) (Hanson, 85).

76. Pacian, *Letter* 6(1) (Hanson, 25).

77. *Contra Novatianum* in Ambrosiaster, *Questions on Old and New* (Literal, 315, 318).

CHRISTIANITY IN THE EAST

The above completes the treatment of the church in the Latin West. Eastern Christendom believed "impeccability is a Divine attribute, and belongs not to human nature; therefore God has decreed that pardon should be extended to the penitent, even after many transgressions."[78]

Bishop Dionysius of Alexandria wrote in a letter that various local churches throughout Anatolia and the Levant had eventually rejected the Novatianists' principle that the church could not absolve from apostasy and some other sins, thus indicating support for the position of Cyprian and his colleagues.[79]

Bishop Eusebius of Emesa in Syria (died circa 359 CE) devoted a homily to demonstrating that sins after baptism could be forgiven. Judging by his arguments and the very fact he thought it necessary to preach on the subject, it appears that even at this late date, some Christians doubted and even denied there could be remission and needed to be convinced.[80]

Shortly before Ambrose, Aphrahat, in the marches between Persia and the Roman Empire, produced an exhortation to repentance that concentrated on baptized Christians. It quoted extensively from Scripture, mainly the Old Testament, treating the two testaments as equally authoritative for his message. He applied them mainly to postbaptismal sins and drew no distinction from prebaptismal. In particular, his *Demonstration* 7.23 (336–337 CE) speaks of the forgiveness of God to all sorts of sinners, not differentiating between baptized and unbaptized, and applied only to a person who was already inside the church. In a similar work, Basil the Great taught that repentance in itself contains the hope of pardon.[81]

There was general consensus that sins were to be pardoned by the bishops and that the sins of apostasy, fornication, and murder

78. Sozomen, *Ecclesiastical History* 7.16.

79. Eusebius of Caesarea, *Church History* 7.5.1 (*NPNF* 2 1:294).

80. Eusebius of Emesa, *On Repentance.*

81. Basil, *Rule of St. Basil*, question 182.

could be forgiven on earth. The latter was a major development, but we do not possess extensive records of the debates leading to the adoption of the principle that major sins could be forgiven, except possibly blasphemy of the Holy Spirit or 1 John's "sin unto death."

There is more evidence for the role of bishops in the west as compared to the east, but the principle of who can administer penitence appears to apply in both regions.

REFINEMENT IN THE WEST

Cyprian assumed that as bishop of Carthage, he was the proper officer to conduct penitential procedures and grant absolution; there was no discussion of this matter except as to the role of martyrs. His correspondence reveals that some penitent lapsed had asked martyrs for letters that they would apply their sacrifice to their reconciliation with God and the church, with the result that for a short time, some penitents thought that forgiveness came through the martyrs with no need for the bishop.[82] This system is known from only three ancient authors in proconsular Africa and Egypt, and Cyprian soon abolished it. Except for clergy whom he delegated, there is no suggestion that anyone else could forgive sins or that Cyprian derived his authorization from his laity or from a universal super-congregational certifying authority.

According to Nathaniel Marshall, "St. Cyprian admitted some to Communion without and against the consent of his people; to whose opinion and request he was, however, in the main, desirous of paying all possible observance."[83] This would argue that the capacity to absolve belonged to the bishop as a distinct officer or occupying a distinct status in the church, and not to congregation members as a unit, but other ancient authors differ on the point.[84]

82. Tertullian, *To the Martyrs* 1; Tertullian, *On Modesty* 22; Cyprian, *Letters* 15, 26, 27; Dionysius, "Letter to Fabius," in Eusebius of Caesarea, *Church History* 6.42.5–6.

83. Marshall, *Penitential Discipline*, 94–95.

84. Burns, *Cyprian*, 13, 23, 32, 81, 99; Marshall, *Penitential Discipline*, 94–95.

There was a core of agreement in early postapostolic times that the church, in the person of an apostle or bishop, possessed sole authority to forgive postbaptismal sins, except perhaps martyrs. Cyprian wrote, "The power of remitting sins was given to the apostles, and to the churches which they, sent by Christ, established, and to the bishops who succeeded to them by vicarious ordination,"[85] and against forgiveness by martyrs and anyone who was not a bishop:

> Only they who are set over the Church and established in the Gospel law, and in the ordinance of the Lord, are allowed to baptize and to give remission of sins; but that without, nothing can either be bound or loosed, where there is none who can either bind or loose anything. Nor do we propose this, dearest brother, without the authority of divine Scripture, when we say that all things are arranged by divine direction by a certain law and by special ordinance, and that none can usurp to himself, in opposition to the bishops and priests, anything which is not of his own right and power.[86]

Much correspondence and some inter-congregational gatherings of bishops considered the issue of forgiveness of postbaptismal sin. One of them in proconsular Africa addressed the case where a priest (probably a bishop)

> rashly at a too early season, and with over-eager haste, granted peace to him before he had fully repented, and had satisfied the Lord God, against whom he had sinned; which thing rather disturbed us, that it was a departure from the authority of our decree . . . before the legitimate and full time of satisfaction, and without the request and consciousness of the people—no sickness rendering it urgent, and no necessity compelling it.[87]

Although rebuking the priest and declaring the action contrary to church law, the gathering nevertheless acknowledged the

85. Cyprian, *Letter* 74.16 (*ANF* 5:394).

86. Cyprian, *Letter* 72.7–8 (*ANF* 5:381).

87. Cyprian, *Letter* 58.1 (*ANF* 5:353).

forgiveness and reconciliation as valid, so great was the authority of any bishop.[88]

THE OFFICE OF THE PRIEST PENITENTIARY

When churchmen opened the gates of reinstatement to all repentant apostates and other backsliders after Decius, the bishops needed to establish a new institution to cope with the hordes of applicants. Socrates Scholasticus records,

> When the Novatians separated themselves from the Church because they would not communicate with those who had lapsed during the persecution under Decius, the bishops added to the ecclesiastical canon a presbyter of penitence in order that those who had sinned after baptism might confess their sins in the presence of the presbyter thus appointed.[89]

Cyprian's *On the Lapsed* 28 indicates that it was usual to go to "God's priests" for forgiveness from idolatry. As soon became common in the East as well, Cyprian deputed presbyters and deacons to receive confessions and to pardon.[90] Eventually, the process was centralized in presbyters or deacons in a congregation or diocese, called the "priests penitentiary." Upon reflection, it is no surprise that sometimes a deacon was chosen: I have written elsewhere that it was largely deacons, rather than presbyters, who officiated as the local clergy in congregations distant from the bishop's city after the transition from the congregational to episcopal polity around the turn of the fourth century.[91]

The title "priest penitentiary" is an unfortunate one because in this era, the word "priest" often referred only to a bishop, but other times encompassed both bishops and presbyters, and with

88. Cyprian, *Letter* 58.1 (*ANF* 5:353).

89. Socrates Scholasticus, *Ecclesiastical History* 5.19 (Knight).

90. Marshall, *Penitential Discipline*, 140; Cyprian, *Letter* 18.

91. David W. T. Brattston, "Chapter 6: Who Became the Local Leaders Under Diocesan Episcopacy?" in Brattston, *Rise of Bishops*, 56–62.

the creation of the office, to specially appointed deacons as well. A notable example is that Cyprian often used the words "bishop" (*episcopus*) and "priest" (*sacerdos* and its adjective form) interchangeably, as illustrated of Bishop Cornelius of Rome in letter 51.[92]

The city of Rome, less populous than the east, had by 309 CE twenty-five such "priests," with the final step in the reconciliation process being conducted by a bishop.[93] The office continued for over a century but was abolished "without any reserve, complaint, or scruple,"[94] beginning in Constantinople in AD 391.

Sozomen records,

> As in supplicating for pardon, it is requisite to confess the sin, it seems probable that the priests, from the beginning, considered it irksome to make this confession in public, before the whole assembly of the people. They therefore appointed a presbyter, of the utmost sanctity, and the most undoubted prudence, to act on these occasions; the penitents went to him, and confessed their transgressions; and it was his office to indicate the kind of penance adapted to each sin, and then when satisfaction had been made, to pronounce absolution.[95]

And Halliburton states,

> This system eventually led to the appointment of presbyters specially commissioned to conduct private interviews and to recommend a suitable length of penance (as Socrates [Scholasticus] records was the case in the time of Theodosius the Great). This was of particular benefit to those whose offence was liable to punishment by the civil law as well as by ecclesiastical censure.[96]

For example, adultery by a woman was a capital offense in secular law as well as a sin.

Nathaniel Marshall gives the full history:

92. Cyprian, *To Antonianus*.

93. Palmer, *Sacraments and Forgiveness*, 77–78.

94. Marshall, *Penitential Discipline*, 37.

95. Sozomen, *Ecclesiastical History* 7.16.

96. Halliburton, "Godly Discipline," 45.

> Now it was the business of that officer to hear the confession of secret sins, and to prepare the party who had been guilty of them for a decent performance of public penance, if that were judged necessary, and in order to it, he directed what should be acknowledged in the face of the congregation; and what was unfit to be there revealed, he advised should be kept in silence. If such an office, or such a practice, had then been judged in all cases necessary, it may seem pretty hard to suppose, that Nectarius should nowhere be censured for daring to abolish them: and therefore it appears to have been at least the opinion of that person in particular, and indeed of that age, which made upon it no remonstrances, that this was an usage in its own nature discretionary, which might either be retained or discontinued, as it should or should not be judged subservient to the use of edifying. Accordingly when a notorious inconvenience ensued upon it, we find it abolished, without any reserve, complaint, or scruple.[97]

Nectarius was bishop/patriarch of Constantinople, whose example for that see started other bishops abolishing the office in areas under their jurisdictions.

Still in ante-Nicene times, probably during the Diocletian Persecution, Methodius of Olympus assumes confession to and assigning rectification of sinful behavior are the duties of the bishop or priest.[98]

According to Canon 32 of the regional Council of Elvira in Spain, sometime in the early 300s but before the Edict of Milan, only a bishop can grant pardon; a presbyter cannot do so except in extreme illness. Hence, the general church made a change and instituted priests penitentiary. At Rome, the bishop conducted the restoration ceremony for decades afterwards.[99] In a discussion of clergy, Jerome, in 373/374 CE, took as undisputed that a presbyter could bind sins.[100]

97. Marshall, *Penitential Discipline*, 37.

98. Methodius, *De Lepra* 6.7, 6.9, 7.4–6, 10.2.

99. Sozomen, *Ecclesiastical History* 7.16.

100. Jerome, *Letter* 14.8 "To Heliodorus, Monk."

Ambrose reaffirmed the position of clergy as occupying a distinct office or status in the church in the penitential process: "This power [to bind and loose sins] has been entrusted to priests alone. Rightly, therefore, does the Church claim it, which has true priests; heresy, which has not the priests of God, cannot claim it."[101] Further, "he who has not received power to forgive sins has not received the Holy Spirit. The office of the priest is a gift of the Holy Spirit, and His right it is specially to forgive and to retain sins."[102] Still further, "God does not make a distinction, Who has promised His mercy to all, and granted to His priests the power of loosing without any exception. But he who has heaped up sin must also increase his penitence."[103] "If baptism is certainly the remission of all sins, what difference does it make whether priests claim that this power is given to them in penance or at the font? In each the mystery is one."[104] Ambrose admitted that "it seemed impossible that sins should be forgiven through repentance, but Christ gave this power to His apostles, which has been transmitted to the priestly office."[105] In quoting Scriptures on God's forgiveness, Ambrose made no distinction between prebaptismal and postbaptismal sins.[106]

A caveat is necessary about Ambrose's judgment that forgiveness, sacraments, and most other ecclesiastical functions are valid only when performed by clergy of the mainline Catholic church. The ancients were divided among themselves as to the validity of sacraments officiated by non-Catholics, as witnessed by the Rebaptism Controversy of Cyprian's time,[107] Canon 19 of I Nicaea, Canon 8 of the Council of Laodicea, and the different treatments of different denominations of heretics in Canon 7 of the First Council of Constantinople. These were at a time when many Christians

101. Ambrose, *Repentance* 1.2.7 (*NPNF* 2 10:330).

102. Ambrose, *Repentance* 1.2.8 (*NPNF* 2 10:330).

103. Ambrose, *Repentance* 1.3.10 (*NPNF* 2 10:341).

104. Ambrose, *Repentance* 1.8.36 (*NPNF* 2 10:335).

105. Ambrose, *Repentance* 2.2.12 (*NPNF* 2 10:346).

106. Ambrose, *Repentance* 1.10.47, 2.2.7. This was a crucial distinction in my book on the matter.

107. Also in Jerome, *Dialogue Against the Luciferians.*

believed that forgiveness was a function only of the properly constituted Catholic church by baptistry or by penance.

Pacian of Barcelona died in the year the office of priest penitentiary began to be abolished. Pacian referred to priests and bishops as the persons to consult for sin and penance as they possess power to forgive on God's behalf. His treatise *On Penitents* 5(1) spoke as if clergy were the only proper officers to prescribe penances and absolve.[108] In 6(2),

> If, then, the power of both baptism and confirmation, which are far greater than charisms, is passed on in this way to the bishops, then, too, the right of binding and loosing was with them. Even though for us, because of our own sins it is presumptuous to claim it, nevertheless God, who has granted to the bishops the name even of his one and only [Son], will not deny this to them as if they were saints and sitting in the seat of the apostles.[109]

More comprehensive is his letter 1.6(1). In it, he chimes in with other early Catholic writers, "Never would God threaten the unrepentant unless he would pardon the penitent,"[110] and counters the arguments against it. He concedes in the opposition contention that only God alone can forgive sins but adds that God forgives through his priests on earth and by his power. He continues that Jesus in John 20:23 would not have said to the apostles, "Whatsoever you shall bind on earth shall be bound in heaven; and whatsoever you shall loose on earth shall be loosed in heaven," if human beings were incapable of exercising power to bind and loose. Pacian adds Christ did not confine this ability to the apostles, as witnessed by the tradition that Christians who were not apostles baptized, conferred the Holy Spirit, and cleansed from sins. The Scriptures also did not show these powers to be conferred on anyone but apostles, but Pacian said the tradition of the church discloses that they were exercised by people who were not apostles and have been passed down by apostolic authority in form, authority, and teaching. The

108. Pacian, *On Penitents* 5(1) (Hanson, 71).

109. Pacian, *Letter* 1 (Hanson, 25).

110. Hanson, 25.

Christian clergy, he wrote, build upon the foundation laid down by apostles. Pacian ended with this: "And lastly, bishops are also called 'apostles,' as Paul relates concerning Epaphroditus."[111] In this way, Pacian linked to the authority of the Catholic bishops of his day to the apostolic and biblical authority to bind and loose from sins.

Question 21 in the *Rule of S. Basil* (of Caesarea), and in the *Shorter Rules* 288, directly asks to whom sins should be confessed. The answer is so vague and oriented in the past as to be of no current value to the questioner, but for the purposes of the present thesis at least, it is arguable that confession should be made to "the saints" without specifying clergy or any particular category of clergy, as in Didache 14.1.

John Chrysostom stands alone in the literature, as he does on other issues regarding postbaptismal sin. I mention him for the sake of scholarly completeness and in case he represented the common practice of Antioch, on which we otherwise possess no contemporary corroboration beside Theodore of Mopsuestia. Quasten writes, "In his six books *De sacerdotio*, in which he elaborates upon the dignity and the duties of the priesthood, he [Chrysostom] mentions seventeen duties of a priest, but never once the hearing of confessions."[112] Nevertheless, Chrysostom took as given that Christian priests can bind and loose from sins.[113]

THE AFTERMATH OF ABOLITION

The office of priest penitentiary was gradually abolished, beginning with Constantinople in 391 CE under Patriarch Nectarius. He ended the office only for the area under his jurisdiction as bishop, but other dioceses independently abolished it soon after, which further indicates that forgiveness and its institutions were local rather than regional or universal. Oscar D. Watkins commented, "So far as appears no opposition was aroused. No schism

111. Pacian, *Letter* 1 (Hanson, 25).

112. Quasten, *Patrology*, 3:479.

113. Chrysostom, *On the Priesthood* 3.5.

was evoked, no mutiny held, no protest made. And it is obvious that an institution which could be thus silenced by a word could not in practice have been of any great account."[114] He continued that the cause and effect of the abolition was "men, in fact, no longer practised the old discipline of Penance,"[115] and "the office was a mere survival of the penitential discipline, and that, as practised, it tended rather to give offence than to furnish edification."[116]

In the very early fifth century Sozomen observed that abolition replaced the old severity and rigor in forgiveness, and that in earlier times Christians had sinned less. They had sinned less, he wrote, out of fear or distaste for confessing their sinful behaviors to a severe ecclesiastical judge and the rigors of the process itself.[117] I would add that other deterrents were the arduous penances and disabilities imposed after confession, which disappeared after 391 CE.

Socrates Scholasticus later complained that whatever the value to the church, abolition took away fraternal correction, the rebuke of another Christian for sins. It led to lack of observance of early church rules not to associate or even eat with backsliders.[118]

After John Chrysostom succeeded Nectarius after his death around 397 or 398 CE, inheriting seven years of an ineffective or absent system of church discipline, he did nothing to rectify the situation or restore the evangelical rigor.[119]

Mortimer related of the ensuing situation among Christians in general:

> The low standard of morality which obtained in respect of certain practices—notably superstition, drunkenness, and fornication—many of the faithful did not consider some grave sins to be sins at all: popular opinion did not condemn them. And for this reason Augustine did not feel himself able to force those who committed these

114. Watkins, *History of Penance*, 357.
115. Watkins, *History of Penance*, 357.
116. Watkins, *History of Penance*, 358.
117. Sozomen, *Ecclesiastical History* 7.16.
118. Socrates Scholasticus, *Ecclesiastical History* 5.19
119. Watkins, *History of Penance*, 358.

> sins to do public penance: partly because their numbers were too great, but chiefly because such a vigorous attitude would have resulted, not in awakening penitence and effecting a cure, but only in alienating the sinner and completely destroying him.[120]

According to a twentieth-century author, penance continued after abolition of the priest penitentiary, but no church official supervised or guided even those backsliders who did confess, nor did anybody deny them the Eucharist.[121] Also in the twentieth century, Poschmann criticized the abolition as "not well advised" and commented that it caused the Eastern churches to lose control over penances through lack of exercising the penitential process, "much to the detriment of moral discipline, and participation in the holy mysteries was left to the conscience of the individual."[122] Poschmann also noted that abolition resulted in "absence of supervision and of official proceedings against sinners."[123] With memorable phraseology, Frend describes the situation: "In Nectarius's last years Church discipline had gone quietly to sleep."[124]

Chrysostom himself did nothing to counter the moral anarchy at the level of the individual layperson but advocated quick and easy forgiveness like that common among most Protestants in our day. Indeed, Watkins opines that his teaching on penance was revolutionary and far ahead of its time.[125] Contrary to what was generally the old order, especially one repentance in a lifetime,[126] Chrysostom's position and advice on forgiveness allowed unlimited sinning and repenting. His *Homily Concerning Almsgiving and the Ten Virgins* 4.19 advised,

> Have you sinned? Enter into the Church and wipe away your sin. The number of times you fall down in the

120. Mortimer, *Origins of Private Penance*, 62.
121. Palmer, *Sacraments and Forgiveness*, 80.
122. Poschmann, *Penance*, 98.
123. Poschmann, *Penance*, 98.
124. Frend, *Early Church*, 210.
125. Watkins, *History of Penance*, 360.
126. Socrates Scholasticus, *Ecclesiastical History* 6.21.

> marketplace equals the number of times you rise up. Likewise, as many times as you sin, repent for your sin; do not become discouraged. And if you sin a second time, repent a second time. Do not be completely deprived of the hope for the proposed goods through indolence. And if you are in the depths of old age and you sin, enter into the Church and repent, because the Church is a hospital, not a court of justice. Here, the priests do not hold you responsible for your sins, but grant you forgiveness. Tell your sin solely to God—"Against you only have I sinned, and done evil before you"—and your sin is forgiven.[127]

In another homily, he says, "If you have sins, do not become discouraged. I never stop saying these things; and if you sin everyday, repent everyday."[128] Socrates Scholasticus alleged that he had said, "Approach, although you may have repented a thousand times," for which Chrysostom was censured.[129] Chrysostom portrayed the path to ecclesiastical pardon as light and easy: "God simply seeks from us one small plea and then grants us the remission of our many sins."[130] He also cited Scripture to illustrate his thesis:

> Did Peter not deny Christ three times? Did he not utter a curse with the third time? Did he not dread the words of an insignificant handmaid? And what of it? Did he require many years to achieve repentance? Not at all; he lapsed and was restored the same night; he accepted the wound and the medicine; he became ill and immediately returned to health.[131]

A twentieth-century Eastern Orthodox author attributes this to him:

> Behold, we have pointed five ways of repentance. First, the acknowledgement of our sins; secondly, forgiving the sins of our neighbor; thirdly, through prayer, fourthly,

127. Chrysostom, *Concerning Almsgiving* (Christo, 39).
128. Chrysostom, *On Repentance* (Christo, 39, 112).
129. Socrates Scholasticus, *Ecclesiastical History* 6.21 (Knight).
130. Chrysostom, *On Repentance* (Christo, 11).
131. Chrysostom, *On Repentance* (Christo, 59–60).

> through almsgiving and charity; fifthly, through humility. Do not delay, but do all these ways each day.[132]

Similarly, in commenting on Ps 141 (Hebrew numbering), Chrysostom taught that the Vespers prayers, which include it, are "a kind of saving medicine and cleansing of sins" of the preceding day.[133] Such easy forgiveness again raises the question of why Christ ordained disciples for this purpose (John 20:22–23).

In contrast to the years-long penances of Anatolia, Chrysostom preached, "The period of five days is time enough to cut away the multitude of your sins if you are sober and watchful and if you pray."[134] In some cases, even a single day sufficed.[135]

In short, the church in the Roman Empire came to the point of holding all sins forgivable after due penances administered by the local bishop or his appointees.

This chapter demonstrates that Catholics entertained a variety of views and followed a variety of practices, all after much deliberation and consulting one another. Differences partly included fundamental concepts of postbaptismal forgiveness, including questions as to which church officers held jurisdiction to do so. Some differences rested on geographical position but even here, there were exceptions. Such variety confirms that there was no one procedure descended through tradition from the apostles nor a general human authority over all Christians in the Roman Empire or even over large parts of it. The differences in practices and concepts demonstrate that each bishop or congregation proceeded on a voluntary basis, with consultation with outsiders helping to make up local minds rather than accepted as binding rules.

132. Coniaris, *These Are the Sacraments*, 142–43.

133. Chrysostom, *Psalms* (Hill, 2:276).

134. Chrysostom, *Against the Anomoeans* 6.30 (Harkins, 178).

135. Chrysostom, *Against the Anomoeans* 6.33 (Harkins, 179).

3

Other Views and Details

THE NEW VIEWS AND procedures did not meet with unanimous acceptance, and there were many exceptions and differences over pardon for sins other than major ones like adultery/fornication, idolatry/apostasy, and murder. Venial or minor sins were usually treated less seriously, while blasphemy against the Holy Spirit or "sin unto death" was treated in a class of its own. This chapter will examine these topics in more detail.

NOVATIANISM

There was opposition to these developments in forgiveness. The Roman presbyter Novatian seceded from the mainstream church, had himself ordained rival bishop of Rome, and gathered some bishops and caused other men who agreed with him to be ordained as new bishops throughout the Roman Empire, such as Novatus and Marcianus of Arles, collectively known as the "Novatianists."

Although there is much literature against Novatian's position on forgiveness of postbaptismal sins, almost nothing about it is from his own hand or from other Novatianists contemporaneous with him. Three of his letters and some monographs on other topics have been preserved, but none of his treatment of reconciliation of the lapsed is extant except in two letters found in the Cyprianic collection. He wrote them while acting leader of the presbyters at Rome during a time it had no bishop and the churches had not yet divided on the issue, and Cyprian himself was still undecided on the matter.

The first letter advised delay and stern treatment of the lapsed so that the apostates would appreciate the process more and the forgiveness could be completely thorough.[1] The second letter on behalf of the presbyters contained phrases such as "the due severity of the divine rigour,"[2] "the vigour of evangelical discipline,"[3] "the severity of the Gospel discipline,"[4] and "it needs no momentary nor over-hasty cure."[5] As previously mentioned, he wrote that it would be

> a false mercy, new wounds should be impressed on the old wounds of their transgression: so that even repentance should be snatched from these wretched beings, to their greater overthrow. For where can the medicine of indulgence profit, if even the physician himself, by intercepting repentance, makes easy way for new dangers, if he only hides the wound, and does not suffer the necessary remedy of time to close the scar? This is not to cure, but, if we wish to speak the truth, to slay.[6]

It called for

> the peace of the Church [to] first be maintained; then, that an assembly for counsel being gathered together, with bishops, presbyters, deacons, and confessors, as well as with the laity who stand fast, we should deal with the case of the lapsed. For it seems extremely invidious and burdensome to examine into what seems to have been committed by many, except by the advice of many.[7]

1. Cyprian, *Letter* 36.1–3.
2. Cyprian, *Letter* 30.2 (*ANF* 5:309).
3. Cyprian, *Letter* 30.1 (*ANF* 5:308).
4. Cyprian, *Letter* 30.4 (*ANF* 5:309).
5. Cyprian, *Letter* 30.6 (*ANF* 5:310).
6. Cyprian, *Letter* 30.3 (*ANF* 5:309).
7. Cyprian, *Letter* 30.5 (*ANF* 5:310).

History shows that members of such councils did not agree with each other, as frequently happens in Christianity.

Over half a century later, a Novatianist bishop told the Emperor Constantine,

> It is not right persons who after baptism have committed a sin, which the sacred Scriptures denominate "a sin unto death" 1 John 5.16 to be considered worthy of participation in the sacraments: that they should indeed be exhorted to repentance, but were not to expect remission from the priest, but from God, who is able and has authority to forgive sins.[8]

There was no agreement on what constituted "a sin unto death." These variations fortify the conclusion that individual bishops always proceeded on their own.

With the paucity of literature supporting Novatian's position, we must warily look to his opponents and one balanced description not written until the fifth century. According to contemporaries in the mainline church, Novatianists told penitent apostates,

> Mourn and shed tears, and groan day and night, and labour largely and frequently for the washing away and cleansing of your sin; but, after all these things, you shall die without the pale of the Church. Whatsoever things are necessary to peace, you shall do, but none of that peace which you seek shall you receive![9]

According to Ambrose, "They affirm that they are showing great reverence for God, to Whom alone they reserve the power of forgiving sins."[10]

A century later, Pacian of Barcelona characterized the Novatianists as holding that "repentance should not be permitted after baptism; that the Church cannot forgive mortal sin; and that, beyond this, by receiving those who sin, the Church itself perishes."[11]

8. Socrates Scholasticus, *Ecclesiastical History* 1.10 (Knight).
9. Cyprian, *Letter* 51.28 (*ANF* 5:335); see also, 55.29.
10. Ambrose, *Repentance* 1.2(6) (*NPNF* 2 10:330).
11. Pacian, *Letter* 3.1.1 (Hanson, 38).

Pacian's letter 3 indicates at length that to counter the biblical and the traditional promises of forgiveness of full and free repentance, Novatianists put forward many arguments and exegeses to exclude certain classes of sinners and types of sin, limiting earthly pardon to only a few minor transgressions. Pacian questioned Novatianism by rhetorically asking, "Can it really be that the devil is able to overwhelm the servants of God and Christ is not able to set them free?"[12]

Long after the heat and height of the controversy died down, the ecclesiastical historian Socrates Scholasticus, in describing contemporary Novatians in part of Anatolia, gave a more balanced description, summarizing the attitudes, both pro and con, in the controversy. In fact, he expressed favorable opinions of Novatianists and their bishops.[13] He recorded that Novatus, a presbyter at Rome,

> wrote to all the churches that "they should not admit to the sacred mysteries those who had sacrificed; but exhorting them to repentance, leave the pardoning of their offense to God, who has the power to forgive all sin." Receiving such letters, the parties in the various provinces, to whom they were addressed, acted according to their several dispositions and judgments. As he asked that they should not receive to the sacraments those who after baptism had committed any deadly sin 1 John 5.16–17 this appeared to some a cruel and merciless course: but others received the rule as just and conducive to the maintenance of discipline, and the promotion of greater devotedness of life.[14]

Note that the decision to accept or reject was one of local option, without a general authoritative body for the worldwide church.

There were thus many factors present on the local level in the deliberations and private thoughts as to how to forgive and

12. Pacian, *Letter* 3.10.1 (Hanson, 50).

13. Socrates Scholasticus, *Ecclesiastical History* 5.21, 6.21–22, 7.12, 7.17, 17.46.

14. Socrates Scholasticus, *Ecclesiastical History* 4.28 (Knight).

reconcile repentant apostates and other sinners with the mainline church. With influences towards both more lenient and more rigorous treatment, Catholics of Cyprian's time opted for a middle ground, especially as against Novatianists and others who advocated stricter standards for pardon or even denied the church could forgive on earth. It appears that in doing so, all sides assumed that the local bishop was the central figure in the process as to the parameters of the content of penances. Although the local "bishop, presbyters, deacons, and confessors, as well as with the laity who stand fast,"[15] set standard outlines, it was the bishop who implemented and conducted them.

THE EUCHARIST AS A MEANS OF PARDON

In or from Antioch, at the time of Chrysostom, Theodore assumed a double approach to reconciliation from postbaptismal sin, and expressed an opinion that would surprise other ecclesiastical authors in his and our own day. He is usually identified with Mopsuestia in Cilicia, of which he became bishop the year after the abolition of the priests penitentiary. In his early time there, or years before, while still a presbyter in Antioch,[16] he wrote that to cure what he termed "great" sins,

> [God] gave us penitence and showed us the medicine of repentance, and established some men, who are the priests, as physicians of sins, so that if we receive in this world through them, healing and forgiveness of sins, we shall be delivered from the judgment to come—it behoves us to draw nigh unto the priests with great confidence and to reveal our sins to them, and they, with all diligence, pain and love, and according to the rules laid down above, will give healing to sinners.[17]

15. Cyprian, *Letter* 30.5 (*ANF* 5:310).
16. Schwartz, *Paideia and Cult*.
17. Theodore, *Lord's Prayer, Baptism, and Eucharist* (Mingana, 6:123).

In contrast, for lesser sins, he said, "We partake of the body and the blood of our Lord, and expect to be changed into an immortal and incorruptible nature."[18] "We ought to believe that by participation in the holy Sacrament [of Communion] our trespasses will be completely wiped out, if we repent and are grieved and afflicted in our mind for our sins,"[19] and "if we do good works with diligence and turn away from evil works and truly repent of the sins that come to us, we will undoubtedly obtain the gift of the remission of sins in our reception of the holy Sacrament, according to the words of Christ our Lord."[20]

Unless *The Sacraments* is a genuine work of Ambrose,[21] with its few earlier slight traces of such an idea,[22] attributing salvific effect to Holy Communion stands alone in the first five centuries of Christianity. It is not included in Origen's list in *Homilies on Leviticus* 2.4.5 for the earlier church. In most ecclesial settings, the Eucharist seems to have been a reward for good behavior rather than a means of reconciliation. Theodore nevertheless reminded his listeners that only Christian priests possess authority to celebrate the Lord's Supper, besides the power to pardon "great" sins.[23] Proposing a means of forgiveness so radically different from other ancient authors illustrates that as bishop, Theodore was truly free from any general or higher authority.

Although W. H. C. Frend alludes to the Eucharist as a means in itself of forgiveness in *The Early Church,* he provides neither references or elaboration.[24]

18. Theodore, *Lord's Prayer, Baptism, and Eucharist* (Mingana, 6:113).

19. Theodore, *Lord's Prayer, Baptism, and Eucharist* (Mingana, 6:119).

20. Theodore, *Lord's Prayer, Baptism, and Eucharist* (Mingana, 6:118).

21. Deferrari (translator) in Ambrose, *Theological and Dogmatic Works,* 265–67.

22. Tanghe, "L'Eucharistie pour la rémission," 173–74.

23. Theodore, *Lord's Prayer, Baptism, and Eucharist* (Mingana, 6:119–21, 123).

24. Frend, *Early Church,* 213.

FORGIVENESS OF VENIAL SINS

This completes discussion of serious or mortal sins. Like the church fathers, this thesis gives proportionately less space to venial sins than mortal ones, because there is less extant literature.

There have been several opinions on the characteristic(s) that distinguish serious or mortal sins from less serious or non-mortal ones. Here, again, there is no general agreement, with various bishops differing from one another. The most helpful and comprehensive treatment is that of Basil the Great. When asked to characterize or distinguish greater sins as a group from venial sins, he replied, "In the New Testament it is impossible to observe this distinction," and ventured that

> generally speaking, however, if we are allowed to speak of a little and a great sin, it can be proved unanswerably that for each man that sin is great which has the mastery of him and that is little of which he is the master, just as among athletes he who conquers is the stronger and he who is beaten is the weaker whoever he be.[25]

Basil based this on the proposition that the essence of any sin is refusal to obey God's command rather a particular act in itself.[26]

Eusebius of Caesarea mentioned "curable sins" and "sins that are lesser in degree."[27] By prescribing different lengths of strictures for different sins or different shades of sins, the ancients manifested that some were considered more heinous than others, although the different lengths prescribed from council to council and writer to writer indicate there was no general consensus as to where lesser sins or degrees of sin fit into any comprehensive spectrum. There were regional differences as well: according to Karl Rahner, "The penitential legislation of the East makes it clear that the notion of capital sins should not be taken too narrowly but means everything that even today would normally be considered

25. Basil, *Shorter Rules* 293 (Lowther Clark, 342).

26. Basil, *Shorter Rules* 293.

27. Eusebius of Caesarea, *Isaiah* 27.1 (Elowsky, 221).

subjectively serious sin."[28] Grueling penances were not always required for sins lesser than apostasy, extramarital sex, and willful homicide, although here there was some variation from bishop to bishop and locality to locality. According to one twenty-first-century commentator, "The author of 1 John and his audience no doubt understood the distinctions between sins 'unto death' and not 'unto death.' The problem is that we are not in a position to reclaim those distinctions with absolute clarity."[29] Thus the vagueness of distinctions in this thesis.

The Catholic churches recognized that there were minor infractions that could be forgiven by more lenient means. In this, they perpetuated earlier authors, as quoted from Tertullian and Origen earlier, under "Sin was Common after Baptism." No scholarly treatment wrote that Christians after the Decian Persecution were noticeably holier than those before.

Gregory of Nazianzus spoke of sins being immediately forgiven upon confrontation with the bishop,[30] which would argue that they were less serious ones.

Despite his preoccupation with mortal sins, especially apostasy, Cyprian held forth that "in smaller sins sinners may do penance for a set time."[31] In contrast to years or decades of penances, he spoke of constant daily sinning, like Tertullian and Origen: "Lest any one should flatter himself that he is innocent, and by exalting himself should more deeply perish, he is instructed and taught that he sins daily, in that he is bidden to entreat daily for his sins."[32] Pacian distinguished idolatry, fornication, and shedding blood from lesser offenses, which "are remedied by the compensation of better works."[33] In pointing out a difference between offenses that can be pardoned only through arduous penitential

28. Rahner, *Penance*, 12.

29. Percer, "Confidence in Christ," 13n46.

30. Gregory Nazianzus, *Funeral Oration on His Father*, 22, 24–26, 33 (McCauley, 136, 138–39, 148).

31. Cyprian, *Letter* 9.2 (*ANF* 5:290).

32. Cyprian, *On the Lord's Prayer* 22 (*ANF* 5:453).

33. Pacian, *On Penitents* 4(2) (Hanson, 74–75).

exercises on the one hand and venial sins on the other, Ambrose specified that "we must repent of our daily faults, but this latter has to do with lighter faults, the former with such as are graver,"[34] and held that for minor offenders,

> It is sufficient they entreat God for their lighter faults, and consider that pardon for weightier sins must be reserved for the prayers of the just. For how could John say that graver sins should not be prayed for, when he had read that Moses prayed and obtained his request, where there had been wilful casting off of faith, and knew that Jeremiah also had entreated?[35]

Halliburton wrote, "Lesser sins, light sins, pardonable or venial sins, were forgiven daily in private and sometimes in liturgical prayer. Hence it is reasonable to say that the majority of Christians in this early period were never subject to the Church's public penitential discipline."[36] Prayer, fasting, and, especially, almsgiving were widely seen throughout Christendom as remedies and purgation for lighter offenses.[37] The earliest of all, which probably predates classifications of sins and institutions for forgiveness from postbaptismal sins, is Simon Peter in Acts 8.22. Marshall's partial summary runs as follows:

> For sins not liable to public discipline, the Father just cited [Augustine], with Pacian and Ambrose, hath shewn us the cure of them by prayers and alms, and by future diligence in good works, which no man, surely, will judge fit to have been imposed upon the sinner under the notion of punishments; though they might be

34. Ambrose, *Repentance* 2.10.95 (*ANF* 10:357).

35. Ambrose, *Repentance* 1.10.45 (*ANF* 10:337).

36. Halliburton, "Godly Discipline," 44; see also, Wagner, "Simple History of Reconciliation."

37. Ambrose, *Repentance* 1.10.44, 2.9.81; Augustine, *Enchiridion* 72–73; Augustine, *Sermon* 351.6 (Hill, 118–33); Augustine in Mortimer, *Origins of Private Penance*, 61, 102; 2 Clem. 16; Cyprian, *Letter* 51.22; Cyprian, *On Works and Alms* 2; *De aleatoribus* 11 in Carroll, "Early Church Sermon"; *Didache* 4.14; Gregory of Nyssa, *Canonical Epistle* (Marshall, 196); Chrysostom, "Homily 3," in *Concerning Almsgiving* 1.5 (Christo, 30); Origen, *Homilies on Leviticus* 2.4.5.

> recommended to him as instances of piety and charity, and of other virtues.[38]

The sum of this heading is that there was no churchwide agreement in distinguishing serious sins as a class from venial ones. It might be cautiously said that like the procedures and lengths for penances, the issue was one of local option, but this cannot be pressed too far.

The lack of uniformity from other places in the Roman Empire was not because bishops did not know of each other and their practice. According to one modern author,

> [Cyprian] both informed and reflected the thinking of many of his contemporary Christians. Because of the relative ease of communication among the local churches scattered about the Mediterranean, and because of Cyprian's habit of writing encyclical letters, having them copied, and making them generally public, both locally on a provincial level, and through other protometropolitan bishops in the Church universal, one can look to his letters as representative of important ideas in wide circulation within the pre-Constantinian Church.[39]

Cyprian himself expressed it thus in a letter to his clergy and laity:

> If any bishops from foreign places, my colleagues, or presbyters, or deacons, should be present, or should arrive among you, let them hear all these matters from you; and if they wish to transcribe copies of the letters and to take them to their own people, let them have the opportunity of transcribing them; although I have, moreover, bidden Saturus the reader, our brother, to give liberty of copying them to any individuals who wish it; so that, in ordering, for the present, the condition of the Church in any manner, an agreement, one and faithful, may be observed by all.[40]

38. Marshall, *Penitential Discipline*, 117.
39. Fitzgerald, "Model for Dialogue," 239.
40. Cyprian, *Letter* 31 (*ANF* 5:311).

Thus, no bishop was isolated or uninformed of what other bishops were doing, which indicates that they did not vary out of ignorance but freely exercised their independence knowingly and voluntarily.

UNFORGIVABLE SIN: BLASPHEMY AGAINST THE HOLY SPIRIT

There remains one sin outside the above categories and in a class all its own:

> Therefore I tell you, people will be forgiven for every sin and blasphemy, but blasphemy against the Spirit will not be forgiven. 32 Whoever speaks a word against the Son of Man will be forgiven, but whoever speaks against the Holy Spirit will not be forgiven, either in this age or in the age to come. (Matt 12:31–32)

> Truly I tell you, people will be forgiven for their sins and whatever blasphemies they utter, 29 but whoever blasphemes against the Holy Spirit can never have forgiveness but is guilty of an eternal sin—30 for they had said, "He has an unclean spirit." (Mark 3:28–30)

> And everyone who speaks a word against the Son of Man will be forgiven, but whoever blasphemes against the Holy Spirit will not be forgiven. (Luke 12:10)

> For it is impossible to restore again to repentance those who have once been enlightened and have tasted the heavenly gift and have shared in the Holy Spirit 5 and have tasted the good word of God and the powers of the age to come 6 and then have fallen away, since they are crucifying again the Son of God to their own harm and are holding him up to contempt. (Heb 6:4–6)
> For if we willfully persist in sin after having received the knowledge of the truth, there no longer remains a sacrifice for sins 27 but a fearful prospect of judgment and a fury of fire that will consume the adversaries. 28 Anyone who has violated the law of Moses dies without mercy

> "on the testimony of two or three witnesses." 29 How much worse punishment do you think will be deserved by those who have spurned the Son of God, profaned the blood of the covenant by which they were sanctified, and outraged the Spirit of grace? (Heb 10:26–29)

> If you see your brother or sister committing what is not a deadly sin, you will ask, and God will give life to such a one—to those whose sin is not deadly. There is sin that is deadly; I do not say that you should pray about that. 17 All wrongdoing is sin, but there is sin that is not deadly. (1 John 5:16–17)

The previous chapters of this thesis do not clarify matters nor disclose how to formulate a guide to distinguish forgivable offenses from this unforgivable or deadly sin. The problem is that there was no known consensus in antiquity. It appears we know this sin was strongly forbidden but not of what it consists. Neither has there been general agreement as to the final step in the process of what constitutes blasphemy against the Holy Spirit or deadly sin, nor even the parameters of such offense. Many opinions or descriptions of this sin were as follows:

- deliberate sin after receiving the Holy Spirit[41]
- lie to the Holy Spirit[42]
- any sin after baptism with laying-on of hands[43]
- deny Christ[44]
- deny that the Holy Spirit is God[45]
- attribute Christ's miracles to demonic power[46]

41. Origen, *De Principiis* 1.3.7.

42. Acts 5:3–10.

43. Origen, *Gospel of John* 28.125. Then follows a quotation of Heb 6:4–6.

44. Luke 12:8–9; Tertullian, *Against Marcion* 4.28.

45. Gregory Nazianzus, *Orations* 31.30 and 34.11.

46. Mark 3:28–30; Pacian *Letter* 3.15(3); Ambrose, *On the Holy Spirit* 1.3.54; Ambrose, *Gospel According to Saint Luke* 7.120.

- refrain from confessing the Holy Spirit[47]
- deny the dignity, majesty, and eternal power of the Holy Spirit[48]
- call Christ "the power of the devil"[49]
- call Christ "the devil"[50]
- test or judge the utterances of a Christian prophet[51]
- Patripassianism, i.e., the heretical belief that it was the Father who was crucified and suffered[52]
- any heresy[53]
- blaspheme God Almighty[54]
- failure to receive the Holy Scriptures, or receiving them ill[55]
- hypocrisy with blaspheming[56]
- blaspheme the Catholic church[57]
- reversion to Judaism[58]
- ascribe to the devil the works of the Holy Spirit, and call Jesus "the power of the devil"[59]
- speak against the Holy Spirit[60]

47. Ambrose, *On the Holy Spirit* 1.3.53.
48. Ambrose, *On the Holy Spirit* 1.3.54.
49. Pacian, *Letter* 3.15(3) (Hanson, 57).
50. Jerome, *Letter* 42.2.
51. *Didache* 11.7.
52. Hippolytus, *Against Noetus* 1.
53. *Didascalia* 25.
54. *Didascalia* 25.
55. *Didascalia* 25.
56. *Didascalia* 25.
57. *Didascalia* 25
58. *Martyrdom of Pionius* 13.1.
59. Pacian, *Letter* 3.15(3).
60. Matt 12:3; Luke 12:10; Origen, *De Principiis* 1.3.2; *Didascalia* 25; Athanasius, *Against the Arians* 1.50.

- disbelieve that sins are remitted in the Catholic church[61]
- preach Arian teachings about the nature of Christ[62]
- "deny the fullness of power to God and to abrogate the eternal substance in Christ"[63]
- deny that Christ is of God or repudiate "that the substance of the Spirit of the Father resides in him"[64]
- "giv[e] some deference to Christ while denying what is most important, that is, while worshiping him as God yet depriving him of communion with God"[65]
- classify the Holy Spirit to be a creature, which is "the forbidden sin" and is the worst impiety and blasphemy possible[66]
- ascribe to an evil spirit instead of the Holy Spirit the fruit of someone who is constant in piety[67]
- try to teach God what God should do[68]
- commit sacrilege like Ananias and Sapphira[69]
- assert that humans should not venerate or revere the Holy Spirit[70]
- disparage the Spirit as a slave or servant[71]
- Montanists and other charismatics attributing their aberrations (in cessationists' judgment) to the Holy Spirit

61. Augustine, *Enchiridion* 83.

62. Athanasius, *Against the Arians* 3.45.

63. Hilary, *Matthew* 5.15 (Williams, 84).

64. Hilary, *Matthew* 12.17 (Williams, 145–46).

65. Hilary, *Matthew* 12.18 (Williams, 147).

66. Athanasius, *Letters to Serapion* 1.33.6, 2.16.4; Basil, *Letters* 113, 159; Basil, *Transcript of Faith*; Basil, *Against Eunomius* 2.33–2.34 and 3.5 imply the equivalent, as does Basil, *Letters* 251 and 188.

67. Basil, *Christian Ethics* 35.1; Basil, *Shorter Rules* 273.

68. Ephrem, *Our Lord* 30.1.

69. Chrysostom, "Homily 12," *Acts of the Apostles* (*NPNF* 1 11:77).

70. Logan, "On the Holy Church," 96.

71. Logan, "On the Holy Church," 96.

- refuse to confess and repent from denial of the veracity of the Bible
- excuse or glory in one's sins
- attribute new heresies and other works of Satan to the Holy Spirit
- struggle against the promptings of the Holy Spirit by baptized Christians
- attribute the manifestations at Pentecostal meetings to a source other than divine
- refuse to repent
- envy of a grace God shows to another person
- presumption regarding the mercy of God
- despair of being saved
- complete rejection of the gospel
- suicide
- unbelief
- failure to accept Jesus as one's savior
- claim for oneself the rights and attributes of God
- past or present association with Satanism
- pride
- cursing an innocent person in the name of the Holy Spirit
- receiving the mark of the beast
- refuse to forgive sins committed against you
- attack Christianity though knowing it is true
- preach Arian teachings about the nature of Christ: reject the belief that Jesus was the Son of God
- indifference to Bible admonitions that conversion requires change of behavior[72]

72. All in Brattston, *Can Sins Be Forgiven*, 55–58.

- "perhaps" it is slighting the Holy Spirit, e.g., by saying the Holy Spirit is not God[73]

Note that heresy was a main theme.

The Gospel of Thomas 44 shows that even Gnostics took literally the import of Matt 12, Mark 3, and Luke 12.

Tertullian said nothing about whether blasphemy against the Holy Spirit is irremissible or how long the lack of forgiveness will last. On the other hand, Gregory of Nyssa, in *Against Eunomius* 2.15, mentioned blasphemy against the Holy Spirit without going on to comment on its forgivability,[74] as did Basil of Caesarea in *Morals* 35.1[75] and Theodore of Mopsuestia.[76] Jerome briefly quoted it without expansion.[77]

While still in the mainline church, Novatian stated the substance of this sin consists of calling Jesus anathema, denying Christ to be the Son of God, uttering words of one's own contrary to the Scriptures, ordaining other and sacrilegious decrees, or drawing up different religious laws.[78] He did not comment on remissibility, but doing so would be contrary to his purpose of listing rather than discussing the Gospels' references to the Holy Spirit.

Cyprian made no relevant comment.[79] Once attributed to him, the third-century *Three Testimonies Against the Jews* 3.28 runs, "Remission cannot in the Church be granted unto him who has sinned against God (i.e., the Holy Ghost),"[80] followed by Scripture proofs. It would appear from Biblindex and the *ANF* indexes for the Cyprianic literature and Novatian that they did not cite Heb 6:4–6 or 10:26–27.[81]

73. Gregory of Nyssa, *On the Holy Spirit.*

74. Gregory of Nyssa, *Against Eunomius* 2.15.

75. Basil, *Morals* 35.1, in *Ascetical Works* 115.

76. Theodore, *Nicene Creed* 101.

77. Jerome, *Galatians* 4.6.

78. Novatian, *On the Trinity* 29 (*ANF* 5:641).

79. Via searches of "Hebrews 6:4–6" and "Hebrews 10:26–27" on Biblindex (biblindex.org).

80. *ANF* 5:542.

81. *ANF* 5:690–99.

Even after the Decian Persecution and the church's acceptance that adultery and apostasy could be forgiven, the patriarch of Alexandria still took literally Matt 12:31, etc. on the unforgivable sin and argued that it can be committed only by Christians, not unconverted pagans or Jews.[82]

The proto-orthodox proponent in *Disputation with Manes* 31 regards the blasphemy to be unforgivable in this world and the next.[83]

In writing about whether Pepuzeni (Montanists) ought to be rebaptized upon conversion to the mainline church, Basil the Great wrote,

> Now the Pepuzeni are plainly heretical, for, by unlawfully and shamefully applying to Montanus and Priscilla the title of the Paraclete, they have blasphemed against the Holy Ghost. They are, therefore, to be condemned for ascribing divinity to men; and for outraging the Holy Ghost by comparing Him to men. They are thus also liable to eternal damnation, inasmuch as blasphemy against the Holy Ghost admits of no forgiveness.[84]

This places Basil among Christian writers who took the stricter view and applied Matt 21:31, etc. in full force as still applying in the fourth century. In his *Book on the Holy Spirit* 18.46, Basil repeated it as still in effect but did not comment on this: "All manner of sin and blasphemy shall be forgiven unto men: but the blasphemy against the Holy Ghost shall not be forgiven unto men."[85] And at 29.75, he wrote, "To me nothing is more fearful than failure to fear the threats which the Lord has directed against them that blaspheme the Spirit."[86] At 28.70, Basil outrightly repeated the warning: "For blasphemy against the Holy Ghost there is no forgiveness,"[87] and at 30.79,

82. Theognostus, *Seven Books of Hypotyposes*.

83. Archelaus, *Disputation with Manes* 31 (*ANF* 6:204).

84. Basil, *Letter* 188 (*NPNF* 2 8:224).

85. Basil, *Holy Spirit* 18.46 (*NPNF* 2 8:29)

86. Basil, *Holy Spirit* 29.75 (*NPNF* 2 8:47).

87. Basil, *Holy Spirit* 28.70 (*NPNF* 2 8:44).

> It would truly have been terrible that the blasphemers of the Spirit should so easily be emboldened in their attack upon true religion, and that we, with so mighty an ally and supporter at our side, should shrink from the service of that doctrine, which by the tradition of the Fathers has been preserved by an unbroken sequence of memory to our own day.[88]

On the other hand, the argument of *Contra Novatianum* is to convince Novatianists that all sins are forgivable, through exegeting Matt 12:31, etc. as containing an explicit reference to general forgiveness. As such, forgiveness is available for sins (such as apostasy) against the Father and the Son. This epistle or treatise generally states that the blasphemy consists of attributing the Spirit's cures and miracles to demons or magic, or denying they happened. As with the Pharisees Jesus reproved, it requires a special malice.[89]

Ambrose of Milan offered hope to Novatianists and other sinners, holding that this blasphemy can be forgiven:

> Peter by his apostolic authority condemns him [Simon Magus] who blasphemes against the Holy Spirit through magic, vanity, and all the more because he had not the clear consciousness of faith. And yet he did not exclude him from the hope of forgiveness, for he called him to repentance.[90]

Ambrose expressed the hope that the original blasphemers in Matt 21, etc. would be saved upon repentance.[91] However, in *On the Holy Spirit* 1.3.54, he pronounced it irremissible.

Ephrem the Syrian held that, despite the clear wording of *Diatessaron* 14.31, such sin can be forgiven in the next world after due penance.[92] All the *Diatessaron* says is that it will not be forgiven in the present age.

88. Basil, *Holy Spirit* 30.79 (*NPNF* 2 8:50).
89. *Contra Novatianum* (Litteral, 310–26).
90. Ambrose, *Repentance* 2.4.23 (*NPNF* 2 10:348).
91. Ambrose, *Repentance* 2.4.26.
92. McCarthy, "Ephrem's Commentary on Tatian's *Diatessaron*," 166–68.

At the other extreme, in a book cautioning against blasphemy specifically against the Holy Spirit,[93] Didymus the Blind wrote that blasphemy against any member of the Trinity is unforgivable.[94] Anyone who blasphemes against the Father "will be tortured without relief."[95] He also held forth that blasphemy can be committed by deeds as well as words.[96]

However, as the present thesis has disclosed through examining Christian literature after the second century, all but a few authors espoused a stringently literal interpretation of Matt 12:31–32, Mark 3:28–29, Luke 12:10, and 1 John 5:16–17, at least in theory, without any consensus on how they applied in practice. Although there was concern over the contents of this sin and some authors thought it extremely important, there appears no consensus on so vital a matter. The best the modern scholar can do is list the opinions of various ancient authors. The fact that there was such variety from the second half of the third century to the end of the fourth lends credence to the proposition that similar variety also pertained to other crucial matters and that it was reserved to the opinion of the individual Christian or his/her congregation led by its bishop, including the forgiveness of postbaptismal sins.

Origen tantalizes with his reference: "Some mortal fault finds us which does not consist in a mortal offense, not in blasphemy of the faith which is surrounded by a wall of ecclesiastical and apostolic doctrine but consists in a vice of words or habits."[97] No record or unambiguous allusion to such "ecclesiastical and apostolic doctrine" is otherwise set forth in the extant literature. If it was of this importance, readers should expect to find it many times, as are canons and descriptions of other serious sins disclosed *supra*. It is unlikely that the "doctrine" was so top secret that all Christians with clearance to know it had died without passing it on.

93. Didymus, *On the Holy Spirit* 1, 212–14, 222, 273.

94. Didymus, *Holy Spirit* 272–76.

95. Didymus, *Holy Spirit* 274 (DelCogliano, 226).

96. Didymus, *Holy Spirit* 214. See also, Hein, *Eucharist and Excommunication*, 122.

97. Origen, *Leviticus* 15.2.1 (Barkley, 258).

Or Origen may have been indirectly saying "nobody knows," as a more face-saving way of admitting "I don't know." If access to such knowledge was reserved to the opinion of the individual Christian or his/her congregation led by its bishop, it is more likely that so were other important features of church life, such as forgiveness of postbaptismal sins.

In short, this chapter demonstrates the topic in greater detail by discussing opposition to the new regime for forgiveness, the status of venial sins in comparison to the mortal sins, which form a major theme of this thesis, the exceptions to the general rule, and finer points in general.

4

The Process of Penance

This chapter presents the actual practice of penance, of what it consisted, how long it lasted, who was in charge, and how penance was conducted in everyday life in the world.

ACTS OF PENANCE

Overview

The differences between various parts of the Roman Empire in the specific behaviors, degrees, and lengths of penance are further indications that the frameworks and details of penance and forgiveness were decided locally rather than churchwide. There was a significant lack of uniformity as to the requirements in forgiving postbaptismal sins. Accounts of the penitential exercises and reconciliation were far different in Anatolia from the western empire. This lack of uniformity is true for Syria-Palestine, as the *Didascalia* deals exhaustively with them. However, the *Didascalia* predates Gregory Thaumaturgus by half a century and John Chrysostom, Theodore of Mopsuestia, and Gregory of Nyssa by one and a half to two centuries, leaving much time for change. There is little evidence for Antioch itself and Egypt. Unless the *Didascalia* still governed Antioch, what little there is for the city and its hinterlands may be gathered from the discussions on Chrysostom and Theodore. What is consistent among the *Didascalia*, Chrysostom, and Theodore is that the penitential exercises lasted less time there.

The West

In contrast to the abundance of detail on the necessity of penance, the Cyprianic corpus is relatively reticent about what acts manifest repentance and penitence. Cyprian speaks only of mourning, weeping, and fasting, and entreating the faithful, and says only a little about sackcloth, ashes, or abstinence from particular kinds of food.[1] These are reminiscent of Tertullian's *On Modesty* 5 and *On Repentance* 9 and 11 in the same city, who does include sackcloth and ashes. Cyprian, in *On the Lapsed* 30, asks, "Do we believe that a man is lamenting with his whole heart, that he is entreating the Lord with fasting, and with weeping, and with mourning?"[2]

The Christian Latin poetry of Commodianus originated sometime between Cyprian and the fifth century, variously described as in proconsular Africa or elsewhere.[3] Section 49 of his *Instructions in Favour of Christian Discipline* exhorts,

> Thou art become a penitent; pray night and day; yet from thy Mother the Church do not far depart, . . .in thy state of accusation learn to weep manifestly. . . . I warn those who are wounded to walk more cautiously, to put thy hair and thy beard in the dust of the earth, and to be clothed in sackcloth.[4]

Ambrose of Milan's *On Repentance* is replete with descriptions of the rigors penitents were required to undergo in the West: "confess Him with groans, with cries, and with tears" (1.5.24)[5]; "the

1. Cyprian, *On the Lapsed* 35.
2. Cyprian, *On the Lapsed* 30 (*ANF* 5:445).
3. McHugh, "Commodian," 222.
4. *ANF* 4:212–13.
5. *NPNF* 2 10:333.

tears of the weepers; your eyes cannot bear the coarse clothing, the filth of the squalid" (1.8.37)[6]; "the garments of mourning, and to cease the groanings of repentance" (1.9.43)[7]; "the bread of tears and tears to drink" (1.13.59)[8]; "if communion be postponed two or three times, that he should believe that his entreaties have not been urgent enough, that he must increase his tears, must come again even in greater trouble, clasp the feet of the faithful with his arms, kiss them, wash them with tears, and not let them go" (1.16.90–91)[9]; "what shaking of the inmost bowels . . ., my bowels are troubled by my weeping" (2.6.46)[10]; "you must implore pardon, throw yourself on the earth with tears, and prostrate on the ground move pity" (2.8.69)[11]; "prayer, fasting, and tears" (2.9.81)[12]; "weeping and groaning" (2.9.88)[13]; "if you weep bitterly Christ will look upon you and your guilt shall leave you" (2.10.92)[14]; and points out that King David "ate ashes for bread, and mingled his drink with weeping. . . . 'Mine eyes ran down,' he said, 'with rivers of water'" (2.10.93).[15] In short, "the world must be renounced; less sleep must be indulged in than nature demands; it must be broken by groans, interrupted by sighs, put aside by prayers; the mode of life must be such that we die to the usual habits of life" (2.10.96),[16] with such results as this:

> I have known penitents whose countenance was furrowed with tears, their cheeks worn with constant weeping, who offered their body to be trodden under foot by all, who with faces ever pale and worn with fasting

6. *NPNF* 2 10:335.
7. *NPNF* 2 10:336.
8. *NPNF* 2 10:339.
9. *NPNF* 2 10:343.
10. *NPNF* 2 10:351.
11. *NPNF* 2 10:354.
12. *NPNF* 2 10:355.
13. *NPNF* 2 10:356.
14. *NPNF* 2 10:357.
15. *NPNF* 2 10:357.
16. *NPNF* 2 10:357.

> bore about in a yet living body the likeness of death. (1.16.91)[17]

At the same time as Ambrose, Pacian of Barcelona indicated that the situation was similar further west:

> To weep in the sight of the Church; to mourn our lost life in poor garb; to fast, to pray, to prostrate ourselves; to refuse luxurious delights if someone invites us to the baths; to say, if someone asks us to a feast, "Such things are for the blessed. I have sinned against the Lord and am in danger of perishing eternally. What do I, who have injured the Lord, have to do with feasting?" And in addition to this: to hold the poor man by the hand; to seek the prayers of the widows; to prostrate oneself before the priests; to beg mercy from the interceding Church; to attempt all these first, rather than to perish.[18]

In a slightly later time, the historian Sozomen recorded this:

> Great rigor by the Western churches, particularly at Rome, where there is a place appropriated to the reception of penitents, in which spot they stand and mourn until the completion of the services, for it is not lawful for them to take part in the mysteries [Holy Communion]; then they cast themselves, with groans and lamentations, prostrate on the ground. The bishop conducts the ceremony, sheds tears, and prostrates himself in like manner; and all the people burst into tears, and groan aloud. Afterwards, the bishop rises first from the ground, and raises up the others; he offers up prayer on behalf of the penitents, and then dismisses them. Each of the penitents subjects himself in private to voluntary suffering, either by fastings, by abstaining from the bath or from various kinds of meats, or by other prescribed means, until a certain period appointed by the bishop. When the time arrives, he is made free from the consequences of his sin, and assembles at the church with the people. The

17. *NPNF* 2 10:357.

18. Pacian, *On Penitents* 10.2 (Hanson, 82–83).

> Roman priests have carefully observed this custom from the beginning to the present time.[19]

In short, reconciliation of backsliders with the Catholic church took long periods of humiliation, afflictions, and labor, such that it provided strong deterrence to baptized onlookers to ever sin and crushed the bodies and spirits of penitents to forever remind them not to sin again.

Moreover, western Christianity imposed lifelong disabilities and restrictions even after reconciliation to the church. In the fourth century, the churches believed a penitent remained a Christian of inferior status even after the penance and forgiveness were completed. He was barred from commercial activity, the military, public offices, and sex. It could be that the penitent must not engage in sex for the rest of his or her life, even if married. The penitent was to devote the rest of his life to good works and spiritual exercises. The purpose of such restrictions was to guard the penitent from the temptations attendant upon participation in commerce, etc. To me, this attitude implies that all penitents were regarded as inferior Christians, weaker in character, who were constitutionally more inclined to sin innately and permanently.

There was at least some difference between pre- and post-baptismal sins, for the latter imposed long-term sanctions and requirements the former did not.

Anatolia

Anatolia, especially Cappadocia, Pontus, and Bithynia, had its own distinctions among repentant backsliders, unlike those of the western Mediterranean. Indeed, there was no evidence of their being in force outside Anatolia.[20] The members of the order of penitents were placed into a process parallel to that of catechumens, with teaching, supervision, division into classes of places in attendance at the divine liturgy (kneelers, co-standers, etc.), close contact

19. Sozomen, *Ecclesiastical History* 7.16.

20. Poschmann, *Penance*, 91.

with clergy, and advancement to full communicant status after a number of years. In these grades, they were little different from catechumens preparing for baptism.

As far as the extant documents allow, the Anatolian practice apparently began with Gregory Thaumaturgus's *Canonical Epistle* 11. Scholarly doubts have been expressed about whether this eleventh chapter was written by Gregory. The main scholar of Gregory Thaumaturgus in our day takes a "maximalist" position and accepts Gregory's *Canonical Epistle* as genuine, making no explicit exception for chapter 11.[21] Quasten attributes the epistle to an unknown bishop but raises no doubt about its antiquity, making no explicit exception for chapter 11.[22] Whatever the reservations, we know we are in the second half of the third century.

Gregory may have taken his cue from his own teacher, Origen at Caesarea in Palestine, who wrote of the practice as well known:

> Christians lament as dead those who have been vanquished by licentiousness or any other sin, because they are lost and dead to God, and as being risen from the dead (if they manifest a becoming change) they receive them afterwards, at some future time, after a greater interval than in the case of those who were admitted at first, but not placing in any office or post of rank in the Church of God those who, after professing the Gospel, lapsed and fell.[23]

Rahner also compares penitential periods with the catechumenate:

> The exercises undertaken during the time of penance (fasts, prostrations, exhortations) also show many similarities with elements of the catechumenate. Thus it is not unlikely that a considerable amount of this particular time of preparation served as a model for the organization of the time of penance.[24]

21. Slusser, *Life and Works*, 5, 9.

22. Quasten, *Patrology*, 2:126.

23. Origen, *Against Celsus* 3.51 (*ANF* 4:485).

24. Rahner, *Penance*, 141.

The height of this system of grades or classes of penitence and the severity of the penances was reached or maintained by what are traditionally known as the Three Great Cappadocians: Basil the Great (330–379 CE), bishop of Caesarea; his younger brother Gregory of Nyssa (c. 335–c. 395), who was bishop of Nyssa; and the third was Basil's friend Gregory of Nazianzus (329–389), who was bishop (pastor) of minor congregations and for a short while was patriarch of Constantinople.

The practical ministry of Basil the Great centered around penances, especially the minute distinctions between sins and the length of time for each. He neatly summarized the procedure and terminology thus:

> During the first year they must be banished from prayers, and must weep at the door of the church; in the second year they must be admitted to the state of "hearer"; in the third, to penance; in the fourth, to "standing" with the people, abstaining from Holy Communion; finally, they must be permitted the communion of the good Gift.[25]

He also stated the lengths of time for which the offender was to do penance in his letters 188, 199 (sections 21–47), and 217 (sections 51–84). One specific length of time is in letter 217.58: "The adulterer will be excluded from the sacrament for fifteen years. During four he will be a weeper, and during five a hearer, during four a kneeler, and for two a stander without communion."[26] Judging by the amount he wrote and the minute details and variations of each sin, not only Basil was absorbed by the subject but so also were other clerics of his place and time, for some of his rulings were in response to questions of other churchmen who sought advice for their own congregations or dioceses.

In a letter to a monk on the fruits of repentance, he describes a penance not untoward in his day:

25. Basil, *Letter* 199.22 (Deferrari, 52); e.g., in the case of murder, Basil *Letter* 217.56; for incest, Basil, *Letter* 217.75.

26. Basil, *Letter* 217.58 (*NPNF* 2 8:256).

> You pricked your body with rough sackcloth; you tightened a hard belt round your loins; you bravely put wearing pressure on your bones; you made your sides hang loose from front to back, and all hollow with fasting; you would wear no soft bandage, and drawing in your stomach, like a gourd, made it adhere to the parts about your kidneys. You emptied out all fat from your flesh; all the channels below your belly you dried up; your belly itself you folded up for want of food; your ribs, like the eaves of a house, you made to overshadow all the parts about your middle, and, with all your body contracted, you spent the long hours of the night in pouring out confession to God, and made your beard wet with channels of tears.[27]

Gregory Nazianzus's *Oration* 16.13 opined that all Christians, especially clergy, should enter the church building "in sackcloth and lament night and day between the porch and the altar, in piteous array, and with more piteous voices, crying aloud without ceasing on behalf of ourselves and the people, sparing nothing, either toil or word, which may propitiate God."[28] And in Oration 2.59, he also stated, "We ourselves must further haunt the temple in sackcloth and ashes, prostrated right humbly on the ground."[29]

Gregory of Nyssa's *Canonical Epistle to Letoius, Bishop of Melitine* is a long, in-depth, intensive, and extensive exposition of factors that lead to the sins detailed, grouped and minutely distinguished, and the various traits of personality and degree of contrition commonly encountered, which a bishop is to take into account when using his discretion to assign or lessen a penance. This fortifies the opinion that churchmen of the time had a fascination with sin and repentance. The fact that church fathers thought it good to publish such particulars suggests that the inquiries were new, without a common tradition from the apostles governing all localities.

In Spain, Pacian sought to justify such austerities by reference to the book of Daniel in the Bible itself:

27. Basil, *Letter* 45 (*NPNF* 2 8:149).
28. Gregory Nazianzus, *Oration* 16.13 (*NPNF* 2 7:518).
29. Gregory Nazianzus, *Oration* 2.59 (*NPNF* 2 7:451).

> That king of Babylon, too, forsaken by all, performed penance and was worn out by seven years of squalor. His unkempt long-flowing hair and the wild roughness of his beard surpassed that of even a lion's mane, and his hands, bristling with long curved talons, greatly resembled those of eagles, while he ate grass in the customary way of oxen, chewing again and again.[30]

Egypt

The nearest to an indication for Egypt is in Dionysius of Alexandria's letter on the church's usual treatment of the repentant baptized sinner:

> We counsel him, of his own accord, to humble and abase and lower himself, with a view to his own improvement and also to what is seemly in the eyes of the brethren and irreproachable before those without. If he consent to this, he will be the gainer: but, if he should object and refuse, then no doubt that will be a sufficient ground for a second exclusion.[31]

To me, this is too vague to reconstruct a penitential system in the same detail as those for the West and Anatolia. This is hardly relieved by the legislation of Archbishop Peter of Alexandria, outlined below.

Antioch and Syria

In commenting on Dionysius's correspondence, one modern-day author gives the impression that Alexandria and Antioch possessed a penitential regime for postbaptismal sinners like that of Anatolia, with grades of penitents.[32] On closer reading, this was not the case, and he has confused material from other sources,

30. Pacian, *On Penitents* 81(3) (Hanson, 81).

31. Dionysius, *Letter to Conon* (Feltoe, 61).

32. Hein, *Eucharist and Excommunication*, 337–39.

mainly Poschmann and the Cappadocians. The impression is nowhere corroborated in the ancient works he cites or in Dionysius's other extant writing.

There is no evidence that penitential practice was affected by Constantine's legalization and intervention in the church.

LENGTHS OF TIME IN PERFORMANCE OF PENANCES

From place to place, there were also wide differences in the lengths of time penitents were required to undergo these austerities. According to Mortimer, "The period of the penance varied from a long number of years—a common experience in the days of Tertullian and Cyprian—to the forty days of Lent, which Pope Innocent I seems to regard as the normal duration,"[33] and the days or weeks of *Didascalia* 6. Innocent I became pope in 401 CE.

There were also differences from region to region. Those in Anatolia were prescribed in numbers of years. Although setting out the various stages of penances, the *Canonical Epistle* 11 of Gregory Thaumaturgus does not say how long a penitent is to be in each; such detail comes down to us from his successors. Indeed, each bishop may have invented it afresh in his own day. The Council of Neocaesarea in Pontus and the geographically nearby First Nicene Council Canons 11 to 14 prescribed years or decades, in contrast to the days or weeks of the *Didascalia* 6.

> Canon 22 of Ancyra (314 AD) decrees lifelong penance for willful murder; two to thirty years, divided among the penitential grades, for idolatry and unchastity, in proportion to the gravity of the sins, as determined by the circumstances; for abortion the "earlier law" of lifelong punishment is mitigated to one of ten years (can. 21).[34]

It was similar with Ancyra 4–9, 16, 20–25.

33. Mortimer, *Origins of Private Penance*, 1.

34. Poschmann, *Penance*, 95.

> Similarly, in the Canonical Epistles the sentences are for the most part in the region of several years' penance. Basil, for example, envisages eleven years for murder, and ten for abortion as the highest penalties (Ep. 188, n. 11 u. 2). In the western Church of the same period lifelong penance was still required for particularly grave sins.[35]

Basil stated the lengths of time for which the offender was to do penance in his letters 188, 199 (sections 21–47), and 217 (sections 51–84). As indicated *supra*, letter 217.58 provided that an adulterer was to spend four years as a weeper, five as a hearer, four more as a kneeler, and two as a co-stander without Communion, in all fifteen years without the Eucharist.

Gregory of Nyssa was similar:

> They, then, who would atone for a wilful breach of the Sixth Commandment, should be reminded, that to such, the time of penance must be trebled; no less than twenty-seven years, nine in each stage of penance, being appointed for them; so that, for nine years, they are to continue in a state of absolute and perfect segregation, all entrance within the Church being entirely forbidden them; for other nine years they are to continue in the Station of Hearers, only to stand hearing with the rest of the people, whilst the Scriptures are read and expounded; and in the third and last novennial space, they are to offer up such prayers as are proper for, and allowed to the Prostrate; and thus, at last, are to proceed to the participation of the Holy Eucharist.[36]

This bishop of Nyssa saw this as a softening of the previous discipline:

> If any one should deny his faith in Christ, or revolt to Judaism, Idolatry, Manichæism, or any such like species of impiety; if, moreover, his apostasy were unforced, and if he should repent afterwards and see his error, such a one, according to ancient usage, would stand condemned to penance for his whole life. For he would never be allowed

35. Poschmann, *Penance*, 95.

36. Gregory of Nyssa, *Canonical Epistle to Letoius* (Marshall, 193).

> to join in Communion with the Faithful, but would be obliged to put up his prayers apart from them; and as to any participation of the Sacred Elements, he would be quite debarred from it; only, in extreme danger of death, he would be permitted to communicate. And if he should recover beyond all expectation, he must return to the same solitary state he was in before his sickness, since it would never be permitted to partake of the Holy Mysteries till the very article of his exit.[37]

Although some scholars regard western Christendom as more forgiving and assigning lighter penances, the Council of Elvira in Spain prescribed quite severe lengths of suspensions from the Eucharist. Among the shorter terms was one year for gambling (Canon 79), and three years for an employer beating her servant to death without intending to kill, five years if intended (Canon 5). Some forms of adultery were assigned ten years penance. Although ten years were assigned to only six offenses (Canons 22, 46, 59, 64, 70, 72), the Council was lavish in the number of offenses for suspending Communion until the death bed (Canon 16), and not even then for fourteen other sins. Like other western churches, these were straight denials of Communion, without placing penitents into categories or stages, or specifying the expected behaviors in penance, as the Anatolian churches did. On the whole, the lengths and severity of Elvira's penances resemble those of the East rather than the more lenient West, which indicates reconciliation was a local rather than regional matter.

At Alexandria during the Diocletian Persecution, the *Penitential Canon* of its archbishop Peter was mild compared to the situation in Anatolia: between six months and four years' addition to a previous penance. He never prescribed delaying excommunication until the penitent's deathbed.[38]

Except for Chrysostom (see *infra*), the shortest minimum durations of penances are found in the *Apostolic Constitutions*: "two,

37. Gregory of Nyssa, *Canonical Epistle to Letoius* (Marshall, 188).

38. Quasten, *Patrology*, 2:116.

three, five, or seven weeks,"[39] like the *Didascalia* 6. In addition, there were penitential periods of shorter, unspecified duration:

- Elvira Canon 21: "for a brief time" (for failure to attend church for three Sundays)
- Arles Canon 12: "excluded from fellowship for a considerable period of time" (for marrying unbelievers)
- Council of Laodicea (c. 363 CE) Canon 1: "a short period" (for marriage after the death of a spouse)
- Council of Laodicea Canon 9: "excommunicated for a time" (for frequenting cemeteries) without stated lengths for other offences
- Sozomen 7.16 on Rome: "a certain period appointed by the bishop"

Presumably, the bishop of the individual penitent would be the sole judge of the length of these nonspecific periods.

On the other hand, two twentieth-century authors raised doubts about whether the lengths of penances were in practice for as long as the canons provided, and whether they applied to more than a small geographical area. Watkins strongly asserts that the regimented and severe Cappadocian penitential grades and practices were never in force at Constantinople, Antioch, or the churches in the *Didascalia* (Syria).[40] However, his arguments are from silence and confuse absence of evidence as evidence of absence. Then again, we have no evidence for or against them. There is mere silence. Our conclusions can be derived only from writings of later periods, such as those of John Chrysostom because of his leadership of both Antioch and Constantinople, if we assume he was not an innovator or eccentric—which is not out of the question. Credence for this assumption about Chrysostom comes from our vast and detailed knowledge of contemporary penitential practices in Rome and Carthage and the West generally, which shared

39. *Apostolic Constitutions* 16 (Haslehurst, 149).

40. Watkins, *History of Penance*, 257–59, 330–32, 346, 349.

some features of his, but fewer of the Cappadocians. Poschmann, the other twentieth-century author, opined,

> The importance of these four penitential stations (στάσεις) has often been exaggerated. The only evidence for them comes from Asia Minor, and they were unknown in the West. From the middle of the fifth century ancient oriental canons, which presupposed the stations, were occasionally drawn upon in the West for the assessment of penance for particularly grave sins. However, these were only exceptional cases, and the canons were suitably adapted to Western penitential law, which only recognized one grade for the whole period of penance from its reception right up to reconciliation. . . . The immediate consequence of this was the postponement of penance for as long as possible. The Church had to be content with this; even herself recommend this practice within certain limits; and indeed absolutely prohibit the admission of young people to penance.[41]

Because the church thought that the young were more open to temptation to sin, especially to sexual sins, and would be in a worse state after formal penance, with its lifelong restrictions and, according to some authors, without subsequent forgiveness, the clergy did not want the one chance at a full reconciliation to be squandered, for it was common opinion among many of them that it was available only once; there was no third chance. The young were regarded as more constitutionally susceptible to sexual temptations and could easily sin again in this regard. More reliable indications, but of lesser length, are discussed under Theodore of Mopsuestia.

Such wide variations serves to highlight that penitence was regarded as a local matter, either of a diocese or even a single parish.

41. Poschmann, *Penance*, 91, 107.

LATITUDES IN PENITENTIAL PRACTICE: THE (LACK OF) INFLUENCE OF COUNCILS

The statement in Sozomen 7.16 to "prescribed means, until a certain period appointed by the bishop" indicates why there was no uniformity from geographic region to geographic region for either the sins, expected austerities, or length of penances, despite the attempts of councils of bishops to standardize them. A modern author opined, "This is probably due to the fact that the mind of the Church on larger issues was already made up, and that the amount of penance to be done for more trivial offences was left to the local authorities."[42] This alters the correctness of von Campenhausen's comment that the council fathers of the early centuries misdirected themselves as to what was important: "It is remarkable that while the christological controversy was being pursued with passion in the field of objective dogma there should be such uncertainty and ambiguity in the confession of Christ on a point of such practical importance."[43] My conjecture is that they considered the issue of postbaptismal sins to be already settled, in the discretion of the individual bishop, or a matter of local option,[44] and there was no need for further discussion or councils for the purpose. Cyprian stated this explicitly.[45] I am fortified in this opinion by a reference in Jerome,[46] and the circumstance that what some bishops in the Province of Africa would consider remissible and bishops in other places would not vary from place to place, even in pre-Decian times.[47]

Gregory of Nyssa mentions the variation over time, with attention to the Anatolian divisions in classes:

> But then, here, likewise, as in the former cases, the officer who executes this Church power should have a due

42. Haslehurst, *Penitential Discipline*, 143, on Council of Laodicea.
43. von Campenhausen, *Ecclesiastical Authority*, 298.
44. Socrates Scholasticus, *Ecclesiastical History* 4.28.
45. Cyprian, *Letter* 55.21.
46. Jerome, *Dialogue Against the Luciferians* 25.
47. Cyprian, *Letter* 50.21.

> regard to the behaviour of the person under Censure, so as to shorten the time of it, as he shall judge to be expedient; and thus, instead of nine years under each stage, to assign him eight, seven, or five, accordingly as he shall observe the degree of his penitence and compunction to compensate for the time in which he should have lain under it, or to exceed the measures of their diligence, who, in a longer time, make less riddance of the work allotted to them.[48]

He also confirms that the issues were in the discretion of the local bishop:

> The disposition of the party should come into the account; that if his compunction appear to be real and cordial, the precise number of years should not too rigorously be insisted on; but that he should sooner be restored to all Church privileges by shortening the time of his penance and segregation.[49]

Basil of Caesarea wrote similarly in regard to monastic communities as pardoners:

> Q: The brothers say: What penalties must be used in the brotherhood for the discipline of those who sin? R: Basil says: Through the testing by those appointed to headship, let the penalties be determined with discernment in regard to all the circumstances and the time and the manner of the complaint, in proportion to the body's stature and the soul's instruction, and in proportion to the particular kind of sin, and the severity of reproof in proportion to the insolence of one who is a stranger to sobriety. So let every censure be weighed with the integrity that is from Christ.[50]

These are all judgment calls for the cleric hearing the confession. The fact that bishops were still asking each other and discussing the details of penances after three and a half centuries of the

48. Gregory of Nyssa, *Canonical Epistle to Letoius* (Marshall, 193).
49. Gregory of Nyssa, *Canonical Epistle to Letoius*, (Marshall, 194).
50. Basil, *Questions of the Brothers* 177 (Silvas, 179).

church forgiving sins in itself indicates that there were no universal rules on penances and absolution and no churchwide body that could enact or enforce such rules.

Given the wide discretion accorded to bishops and the utter lack of uniformity as to which postbaptismal sins may be forgiven and how, I conclude that the content and lengths of penances prescribed by inter-congregational councils were voluntary guidelines and assistance in judging rather than hard-and-fast rules binding on the bishops and priests they had appointed to administer penitence (priests penitentiary). There would be a flaw in this argument if the councils pronounced anathemas in connection with penances and their processes. This flaw disappears once it is observed that the councils never pronounced anathemas, excommunications, or other ecclesial punishments on bishops who did not comply with their prescriptions for penances, nor did they nullify the forgiveness. They refrained on the issue of penance despite readily imposing sanctions for violations of their other legislation:

During the Donatist controversy, a synod at Rome in 313 CE nullified the deposing of a cleric and affirmed the ordinations of others as part of a general policy.

Council of Arles 314 CE Canon 13 (12) excluded usurious clergy from fellowship. Canon 14 deposed *traditores* of the Scriptures but held their ordinations of others to be valid.[51] Canon 15 states, "Concerning those who have falsely accused their brothers, be it resolved that they not be given fellowship as long as they live."[52] Canon 22 does mention apostates who never applied for penance or forgiveness until their deathbeds, to whom the working of penitence would not apply.[53]

Ancyra Canon 4 deposed clergy for refusal to eat meat/flesh; Canon 18 deposed bishops who invade another bishop's parish. Neocaesarea Canon 1 deposed presbyters who marry after ordination. Canon 2 excommunicated women who marry twice. The Canons of the Council of Gangra contain many anathemas

51. Haslehurst, *Penitential Discipline*, 137.

52. Council of Arles, *Canons* 15.

53. Council of Arles, *Canons* 22.

for various heretical practices but address none of the topics in this thesis. The Synod of Antioch in Encaeniis AD 325 assembled churchmen from the provinces of Coele-Syria, Phoenicia, Palestine, Arabia, Mesopotamia, Cilicia, and Isauria. It dealt mainly with church order. It deposed some clerics and nullified acts done in contravention of its Canons, not concerning penitential procedures.

Canon 9 of Laodicea in Phrygia Pacatiana contains an excommunication of Christians who worship in cemeteries and martyries. Canon 35 anathematizes worshipers of angels. Canon 36 casts clergy out of the church who engage in the occult. Many of the canons of this council deal with quite small points in the conduct of services, etc., but there is no mention of stated lengths of penance.[54]

First Nicaea 10 deposed clergy who were ordained through officiating bishops' ignorance of the candidates' prior apostasy. Canon 16 excommunicated all those who helped a man to be ordained without the consent of his bishop and nullified the ordination. Canons 17 and 18 deposed usurers and deacons acting above their stations at Divine Liturgy. Canon 13 urges, as "an ancient canonical law," that a dying man "should not be deprived of the last and most necessary Viaticum";[55] on other points, however, the regulations are extremely severe.

In 347 CE, Council of Sardica was wholly involved with appointment, powers, and proper conduct of bishops. Canon 15 nullifies ordinations wherever someone becomes bishop of another parish without consent of his own bishop. Canons 18 and 19 condemn ordination without the consent of a man's bishop and nullify such ordinations.

The letter of the Synod of Antioch (325 CE) did not deal with forgiveness of postbaptismal sins. Milan 345 CE anathematized people whom the attendees considered heretics. Valentia 374 CE forbade the ordination in future of men who have been twice married, whether before or after baptism, or who have married

54. Haslehurst, *Penitential Discipline*, 143, on the Council of Laodicea.

55. *NPNF* 2 14:29.

widows, but it did not insist upon the deposition of those who had been already ordained.[56] First Constantinople 4 contains nullifications of ordinations, but not for clergy because of irregularity in their conduct of penance.

In short, the Catholic church nullified a bishop's ordinations only for an issue other than a bishop's conduct of penance. In no extant case that I found did a council discipline, threaten to discipline, or provide for discipline of clerics who violated its pronouncements on the structure, conditions, or other specifics of conducting penances or procedures for postbaptismal sins. Many of them provided a wide latitude and discretion to bishops to shorten the time of a penance or otherwise reduce its severity. All this would indicate that their pronouncements on manifestations of penitence were mere advice, or suggested guidelines, rather than firm rules or obligatory.

Until the Peace of the Church, inter-congregational councils deliberated mainly on penitence. From 314 CE onwards, their main business was the regulation and prerogatives of clergy, especially bishops. This continued in part after I Constantinople, overshadowed by definitions of doctrines and combat of heresies. A disproportionate number of councils dealt with the character and actions of Athanasius of Alexandria. So independent were bishops from councils that Athanasius felt free to ignore the decision of a synod when setting the date for a particular Easter for his presbyters and deacons.[57] Indeed, bishops who had been deposed sometimes held a later council of similarly deposed. Some were deposed more than once.[58]

The contradictions and lack of agreement among councils, especially between the East and West, were not because churchmen in one area did not know about the others. According to Poschmann, "By reason of the brisk intercourse between the provinces of the Church, synodal decrees often gained recognition outside

56. Landon, *Manual of Councils*, no. 262 (p. 254).

57. Athanasius, *Letter* 18.

58. Athanasius, *Epistle to the African Bishops* 3, 4, 77.

the jurisdictional limits of the councils."[59] Frequent long-distance travelers, such as Origen and Athanasius, must have noticed some differences if there had been any, as would the attendees of the Nicene and Constantinopolitan councils, who came from all over the Roman world.

Not even an ecumenical council could influence the methods or lengths of penitence. At first sight, Canons 11 and 12 of I Nicaea—and for catechumens Canon 14—legislated on the assumption that only the Anatolian procedures of graded penances were normal for certain mentioned offenses. However, they did not require the Christian West to adopt graded penances lasting years, and there is a startling lack of evidence that there was any such change for the West and overwhelming evidence that it proceeded as before. This confirms that everyone assumed postbaptismal sins and penances were within the sole jurisdiction of local bishops or churches. Actually, the First Council of Nicaea was not universally accepted during its time. It took generations for the public to accept its decision on the main issue for which it was assembled (precise deity of Jesus Christ).

Despite the advice of church councils in the various regions, Christianity in the Roman Empire between 249 to 391 CE was not uniform in what constituted necessary penitential acts, the manifestations of repentance to be demonstrated, the lengths of time they were to be performed, and variations of them, even within geographic regions. All seemed to be a matter of congregational or diocesan option, perhaps even from bishop to bishop in the same neighborhood. The fact that penitential practices were worked out separately in Anatolia and Africa, from scratch and with changes along the way in the latter, indicates that there was no common tradition descended from the apostles or other overarching Christian authority, with each local area or congregational leader proceeding as he or she thought best.

59. Poschmann, *Penance*, 83.

Conclusions

NO DIFFERENCE IN FORGIVING PREBAPTISMAL AND POSTBAPTISMAL SIN

THE ABOVE THESIS LEADS to the conclusion that promises of forgiveness apply equally to pre- and postbaptismal sin. As interpreters of Scripture and an oral tradition from the apostles themselves as how to interpret it, Christians in the third and fourth centuries demonstrated there was no consensus regarding the forgiveness of postbaptismal sins even in the earliest times, and thus, later bishops or congregations or dioceses were free to innovate.

Indeed, some post-Decian authors equally applied the same New Testament verses to all repentances in both categories, opening the promises for pardon of prebaptismal sins to those afterwards. To one man ordained by Gregory of Nazianzus, the matter for monks at the end of our period was more of degree than of kind: "It is easier to purify an impure soul than it is to bring back to health one that has been purified and wounded again."[1]

SYNOPSIS

The earliest successors of Christ and the apostles sinned so much after conversion and water baptism that the churches provided

1. Evagrius, *On Thoughts* (Sinkewicz, 178).

standard routines for reconciling baptized sinners to God and the Catholic community. Different localities developed local conditions as to what, which, how, how long, and when forgiveness would be finalized. As in most developments in Christianity throughout the ages, the changes also produced minorities who did not agree. As for the subject of this thesis, dissenters included much more behavior in their reckoning of what constituted unforgivable sins and denied that some kinds could ever be pardoned on earth.

The church or individuals in it groped from age to age in reconsidering the particular prohibited actions and the manifestations of repentance and sincerity in extending forgiveness for them. The differences among them were not whether they were to be forgiven but the time lengths and penitential actions for doing so. Cyprian, in particular, changed his mind. The issues developed over the ages; they did not emerge full-blown at a particular point in time after the New Testament was written. Considerations included what was to the benefit of the penitent person, the effect of too easy reinstatement on Christians who had remained faithful, compensation to the church for damage to its reputation, and preventing backsliders from contaminating faithful Christians, where some authors regarded sin as a communicable sickness.

The procedures of pardoning serious sins differed geographically from the detailed regimentation and institutionalization of repentance in Anatolia, with different classes of penitents and recommendations of duration in each class, to the more equal treatment generally in force in the West. In most places, regaining the favor of the church and God took years of humiliation, tears, fasting, and afflicting oneself. Some authors assumed that dramatically lesser penances were appropriate for venial sins, such as simple prayer, fasting, and, especially, almsgiving. In a third category from pardonable mortal and venial sins was blasphemy against the Holy Spirit, the unforgivable sin. Although Origen spoke of it as "surrounded by a wall of ecclesiastical and apostolic doctrine,"[2] no indisputable proof has survived, or been adduced for later ages, as to how to identify the substance of this wall.

2. Origen, *Leviticus* 15.2.1 (Barkley, 258).

The methods and content of forgiving postbaptismal sins were matters of purely local option.

WHO COULD FORGIVE?

Without debating the issue, every writer on the subject between 249 and 391 CE assumed that bishops were included as the chief officers to hear confessions, prescribe penances, and grant absolution. This assumption can be first dated to the period when bishops were strictly officers of autonomous congregations, but was fortified after the transition to diocesan episcopacy around the turn of the fourth century and, especially, during the reign of Constantine.[3] Bishops often delegated these functions to deacons and presbyters, known as "priests penitentiary," with the bishops usually reserving public absolution to themselves. The office of a designated priest penitentiary for each bishopric began to be quickly abolished from AD 391. Its abolition led to or accelerated a drastic decline in lay morality and spirituality and in preference to seek reconciliation with the church by other less burdensome penitential methods, if at all.

OUTSTANDING ISSUES

Several issues related to this study remain outstanding: Did Cyprian and the other ancient writers have jurisdiction to pronounce upon, reform, or institute their forms of forgiveness for all time or even for their own time? Did they invent powers for themselves? Could sin be validly forgiven by some other method(s), without the mediation of clergy? Is the distinction between serious and minor sins in writers of the third and fourth centuries eternally valid in that there is no such distinction in Scripture? Since they bear witness to one another and to the pre-Decian writers, did Montanists and Novatianists represent an earlier, more orthodox tradition descended

3. Brattston, *Rise of Bishops*, 24–28.

from the apostles, which the mainline church violated by providing forgiveness for apostasy, fornication, and murder?

CONCLUSION

The questions studied in this thesis in the period of the priests penitentiary (250 CE to 391 CE) among Christians in the Roman Empire were

- whether there was pardon for any sins committed after water baptism;
- whether all sins were considered remissible after baptism, or were there exceptions;
- which actions constituted an appropriate manifestation of sorrow and remorse for sins; and
- which officers of the church held authority to hear and adjudicate confessions of sins and declare them forgiven on earth and in heaven.

The thesis concludes that such questions were decided individually by the local bishop or his diocesan or parish council.

Bibliography

Ad Novatianum, or Treatise Against the Heretic Novatian That the Hope of Pardon Should not Be Denied to the Lapsed, by an Anonymous Bishop. In *ANF* 5:657–63.

Ambrose. *Explanatio Psalmorvm XII*. Recensvit M. Petschenig. New York: Johnson, 1962.

———. *Exposition of the Holy Gospel According to Saint Luke: With, Fragments on the Prophecy of Isaias*. Translated by Theodosia Tomkinson. Etna, CA: Center for Traditionalist Orthodox Studies, 1998.

———. *Expositio Psalmi CXVIII*. Recensvit M. Petschenig. Vienna: F. Tempsky, 1913.

———. *On Repentance*. In *NPNF* 2 10:329–59.

———. *On the Duties of Clergy*. In *NPNF* 2 10:[1]–89.

———. *On the Holy Spirit*. In *Theological and Dogmatic Works*, translated by Roy J. Deferrari, 31–214. Washington, DC: Catholic University of America Press, 1963.

———. *Theological and Dogmatic Works*. Translated by Roy J. Deferrari. Washington, DC: Catholic University of America Press, 1963.

———. *Three Books of St. Ambrose, Bishop of Milan, on the Holy Spirit*. In *NPNF* 2 10:93–158.

Ambrosiaster. *Questions on the Old and New Testaments*. Edited by John Litteral. Internet Archive, July 29, 2018. https://archive.org/details/ambrosiaster-questions-and-answers-on-the-old-and-new-testaments/page/310/mode/2up.

Ammon. "A Letter of Bishop Ammon." In *Koinonia: Pachomian Chronicles and Rules*, vol. 2, written by Pachomian, translated by Armand Veilleux, 71–109. Kalamazoo, MI: Cistercian, 1981.

Ammonas. *The Letters of Ammonas, Successor of St. Anthony*. Translated by Derwas J. Chitty and Sebastian P. Brock. Oxford: SLG, 1979.

Andreassen, Bengt-Ove. "A Review of Theories on the Laestadian Rørelse: On the Academic Construction of Something Extraordinary and Exotic." *Acta Borealia* 34.1 (2017) 70–89. doi:10.1080/08003831.2017.1323482.

Antenucci, Chris. "A History of the Use of the Sacrament of Reconciliation in the Early Church." Medium, Mar. 28, 2018. https://medium.com/@chrisantenucci/a-history-of-the-use-of-the-sacrament-of-reconciliation-in-the-early-church-8d0eaf275faf.

Apostolic Constitutions, or Constitutions of the Holy Apostles. In *ANF* 7:385–505.

Archelaus. *Disputation with Manes.* In *ANF* 6:179–235.

Asterius. *Ancient Sermons for Modern Times.* Translated by Edgar J. Goodspeed and Galusha Anderson. New York: Pilgrim, 1904.

Athanasius. *Contra Gentes, or Against the Heathen.* In *NPNF* 2 4:[4]–30.

———. *De Decretis, or Defence of the Nicene Definition.* In *NPNF* 2 4:482–536.

———. *De Sententia Dionysii, or On the Opinion of Dionysius.* In *NPNF* 2 4:541–59.

———. *Discourse Which the Holy Patriarch, Apa Athanasius, Archbishop of Kakote, Pronounced Concerning the Soul and the Body.* Translated by Ernest Alfred Wallis Budge. Wikisource. https://en.wikisource.org/wiki/Coptic_homilies_in_the_dialect_of_Upper_Egypt/Sermon_9.

———. *Encyclical Epistle to the Bishops Throughout the World.* In *NPNF* 2 4:377–88.

———. *Epistle to the African Bishops.* In *Later Treatises of S. Athanasius, Archbishop of Alexandria: With Notes, and an Appendix on S. Cyril of Alexandria and Theodoret*, 23–42. Oxford: J. Parker, 1881.

———. *Letter to Marcellinus on the Interpretation of the Psalms.* Theology and Ethics. https://www.theologyethics.com/2016/08/22/the-letter-of-athanasius-to-marcellinus-on-the-interpretation-of-the-psalms/.

———. *Letter to the Bishops of Egypt.* In *NPNF* 2 4:643–66.

———. *Letters 1–64.* Translated by Archibald Robertson. In *Nicene and Post-Nicene Fathers*, second series, vol. 4, edited by Philip Schaff and Henry Wace. Buffalo, NY: Christian Literature, 1892. Revised and edited for New Advent by Kevin Knight. https://www.newadvent.org/fathers/2806.htm.

———. *Letters Concerning the Holy Spirit.* London: Epworth, 1951.

———. *Life of Antony.* In *NPNF* 2 4:572–640.

———. *On the Incarnation of the Word.* In *NPNF* 2 4:258–335.

———. "San Atanasio: tratado de salud dirigido a una virgen." In *Las virgenes cristianas de la iglesia primitiva: Estudio histórico-ideológico seguido de una antología de tratados patrísticos sobre la virginidad.* Translated by Francisco de B. Vizmanos. Madrid: Editoral Católica, 1949.

———. *Third Discourse Against the Arians.* In *NPNF* 2 4:827–99.

Augustine. *Earlier Writings.* Edited by J. H. S. Burleigh. Louisville: Presbyterian, 2020.

———. *Enchiridion.* In *NPNF* 1 9:175–260.

———. *Letters, Volume 1 (1–82).* Translated by Sister Wilfrid Parsons. Fathers of the Church. Washington, DC: Catholic University of America Press, 2008.

———. *Sermons on Various Subjects*. In *The Works of Saint Augustine: A Translation for the 21st Century*, edited by John E. Rotelle, translated by Edmund Hill, III/10:341–400. Hyde Park, NY: New City, 1995.

Basil. *Against Eunomius*. Translated by Mark DelCogliano and Andrew Radde-Gallwitz. Washington, DC: Catholic University of America Press, 2011.

———. *Ascetical Works*. Translated by M. Monica Wagner. Washington, DC: Catholic University of America Press, 1950. ProQuest Ebook Central.

———. *The Ascetic Works of Saint Basil*. Translated by W. K. Lowther Clarke. London: SPCK, 1925.

———. *Christian Doctrine and Practice*. Translated by Mark DelCogliano Yonkers. Yonkers, NY: St. Vladimir's Seminary Press, 2012.

———. *Christian Ethics*. Translated by Jacob Van Sickle. Yonkers, NY: St. Vladmir's Seminary Press, 2014.

———. *De Spiritu Sancto, or Book on the Holy Spirit*. In *NPNF* 2 8:1–50.

———. *Epistles*. In *NPNF* 2 8:109–327.

———. *Exegetic Homilies*. Translated by Agnes Clare Way. Washington, DC: Catholic University of America Press, 1963.

———. "Exhortation to Baptism." In *A Treatise on Baptism: With an Exhortation to Receive It. Translated from the Works of St. Basil the Great, to Which Is Added a Treatise on Confirmation*, by Basil and Francis Patrick Kenrick, 225–41. Philadelphia: M. Fithian, 1843.

———. *Fasting and Feasts*. Translated by Susan R. Holman and Mark DelCogliano. Yonkers, NY: St. Vladimir's Seminary Press, 2013.

———. *Herewith Begins the Morals*. In *Ascetical Works*, 71–205. Washington, DC: Catholic University of America Press, 1950.

———. "Homily 16 on 'In the Beginning Was the Word.'" Translated by Austin Dominic Litke. *Logos: A Journal of Catholic Thought & Culture* 26.2 (2023) 151–60.

———. *Letter 199, to Amphilochius, Concerning the Canons*. In *Letters, Volume 2 (186–368)*, translated by Roy J. Deferrari, 47–62. Washington, DC: Catholic University of America Press, 1955.

———. *Letters, Volume 1 (1–185)*. Translated by Roy J. Deferrari. Washington, DC: Catholic University of America Press, 1951.

———. *Letters, Volume 2 (186–368)*. Translated by Roy J. Deferrari. Washington, DC: Catholic University of America Press, 1955.

———. *Preface on the Judgment of God*. In *Ascetical Works*, translated by M. Monica Wagner, 37–55. Washington, DC: Catholic University of America Press, 1950. ProQuest Ebook Central.

———. *The Rule of St. Basil in Latin and English: A Revised Critical Edition*. Translated by Anna M. Silvas. Collegeville, MN: Liturgical, 2013.

———. *Shorter Rules*. In *The Ascetic Works of Saint Basil*, 229–351. Translated by W. K. Lowther Clark. London: SPCK, 1925.

———. *Social Justice*. Translated by C. Paul Schroeder. Crestwood, NY: St. Vladimir's Seminary Press, 2009.

———. *A Transcript of the Faith as Dictated by Saint Basil, and Subscribed by Eustathius, Bishop of Sebasteia* (*Letter* 125). In *NPNF* 2 8:194–96.

Bauerschmidt, John C. "The Godly Discipline of the Primitive Church." *Anglican Theological Review* 94.4 (2012) 685–94.

Beane, Larry. "Apostolic Succession in the Roman Catholic and Lutheran Churches." *Gottesdienst Crowd* (podcast), Apr. 26, 2021. https://www.podbean.com/media/share/pb-n5xrb-10157f3?utm_campaign=embed_player_stop&utm_medium=dlink&utm_source=embed_player.

Berington, Joseph, and John Kirk. *The Faith of Catholics on Certain Points of Controversy, Confirmed by Scripture, and Attested by the Fathers of the Five First Centuries of the Church*. London: Printed for Joseph Booker, 1830.

Bévenot, Maurice. "The Sacrament of Penance and St. Cyprian's *De Lapsis*." *Theological Studies* 16.2 (1955) 175–213.

Blatz, Beate, trans. "The Coptic Gospel of Thomas." In *New Testament Apocrypha*, edited by Wilhelm Schneemelcher, English translation edited by R. McL. Wilson, 1:117–129. Revised ed. Cambridge, UK: James Clarke, 1991.

Boda, Mark J., and Gordon T. Smith. *Repentance in Christian Theology*. Collegeville, MN: Liturgical, 2006.

Booth, Edward. "Penance in the Early Church." *Life of the Spirit* 14.157 (1959) 18–25. http://www.jstor.org/stable/43705467.

Botha, Philippus J. "Ephrem the Syrian's Hymn 'On the Crucifixion 4.'" *Hervormde Teologiese Studies* 71.3 (2015) 1–8.

Boyd, Darce R. "Translation of Homilia in Divites by Basil of Caesarea with Annotation and Dating." PhD diss., Temple University, 2014.

Bradley, James E., and Richard A. Muller. *Church History: An Introduction to Research Methods and Resources*. Grand Rapids: Eerdmans, 2016.

Brattston, David W. T. *Apostolic Succession: An Experiment That Failed*. Eugene, OR: Resource, 2020.

———. *Can Sins Be Forgiven After Baptism?* N.p.: St. Polycarp, 2019.

———. "The Forgiveness of Postbaptismal Sin in Ancient Christianity." *Churchman: A Journal of Anglican Theology* 105.4 (1991) 332–40.

———. *Papal Supremacy: Quotations and Commentaries*. N.p.: St. Polycarp, 2018.

———. *The Rise of Bishops: From Parish Leaders to Regional Governors*. Eugene, OR: Wipf & Stock, 2021.

———. *Traditional Christian Ethics*. 4 vols. Bloomington, IN: WestBow, 2014.

Bray, Gerald. *Anglicanism: A Reformed Catholic Tradition*. Bellingham, WA: Lexham, 2021. ProQuest Ebook Central.

Bryant, Joseph M. "Wavering Saints, Mass Religiosity, and the Crisis of Postbaptismal Sin in Early Christianity: A Weberian Reading of the Shepherd of Hermas." *European Journal of Sociology* 39.1 (1998) 49–77. http://www.jstor.org/stable/23997597.

Budge, Ernest Alfred Wallis, trans. "Coptic Homilies in the Dialect of Upper Egypt/Introduction." Wikisource, Oct. 8, 2022. https://en.wikisource.org/wiki/Coptic_homilies_in_the_dialect_of_Upper_Egypt/Introduction.

Burggraf, Andrew T. "A Historical Study of the Catechumenate and Its Implications for Discipleship in 21st Century Churches." EdD diss., Southeastern Baptist Theological Seminary, 2014.

Burns, J. Patout Jr. *Cyprian the Bishop*. Oxford: Taylor & Francis, 2001.

Carroll, Scott T. "An Early Church Sermon Against Gambling (CPL 60)." *Second Century: A Journal of Early Christian Studies* 8.2 (1991) 83–95.

Carter, Robert E. "A Greek Homily on the Temptation (CPG 4906) by Severian of Gabala: Introduction, Critical Edition, and Translation." *Traditio* 52 (1997) 47–71.

Catechism of the Catholic Church. 2nd ed. Washington, DC: United States Catholic Conference, 2000.

Chrysostom, John. *Commentary on the Psalms*. 2 vols. Translated by Robert C. Hill. Brookline, MA: Holy Cross Orthodox, 1998.

———. "English Translation of *de laudibus sancti Pauli 1–7* [In praise of Saint Paul]." In *The Heavenly Trumpet: John Chrysostom and the Art of Pauline Interpretation*, written by Margaret M. Mitchell, 440–87. Louisville: Westminster John Knox, 2002.

———. *Homilies Against the Anomoeans*. In *John Chrysostom, On the Incomprehensible Nature of God*, translated by Paul W. Harkins. Washington, DC: Catholic University of America Press, 1984.

———. *Homilies Concerning the Statues*. Vol. 12. In *NPNF* 1 9:418–25.

———. *Homilies on Hebrews*. In *NPNF* 1 14:363–522.

———. *Homilies on Acts of the Apostles*. In *NPNF* 1 11:1–328.

———. *Homilies on the Beginning of Acts*. In "Introducing the Acts of the Apostles: A Study of John Chrysostom's on the Beginning of Acts," written by Michael Bruce Compton, [247]–312. PhD. diss., University of Virginia, 1996.

———. *Homilies on the Epistle to Titus*. In *NPNF* 1 13:519–43.

———. *Homilies on the First Epistle of Paul to the Corinthians*. In *NPNF* 1 12:1–269.

———. *Homilies on the First Epistle of St. Paul the Apostle to the Thessalonians*. In *NPNF* 1 13:323–27.

———. *Homilies on the Second Epistle of Paul to the Corinthians*. In *NPNF* 1 12:271–420.

———. "Homily 8." In *Homilies on the First Epistle of St. Paul the Apostle to the Thessalonians*. In *NPNF* 1 13:355–61.

———. *Homily Concerning Almsgiving and the Ten Virgins*. In *On Repentance and Almsgiving*, translated by Gus George Christo, 28–42. Washington, DC: Catholic University of America Press, 1998.

———. *On Repentance and Almsgiving*. Translated by Gus George Christo. Washington, DC: Catholic University of America Press, 1998.

———. *On the Incomprehensible Nature of God*. Washington, DC: Catholic University of America Press, 1984.

———. *Panégyriques de S. Paul*. Edited and translated by Auguste Piédagnel. Paris: Editions du Cerf, 1982.

———. *Treatise Concerning the Christian Priesthood*. In *NPNF* 1 9:33–83.

Church of Jesus Christ of Latter-Day Saints. "Blaspheme, Blasphemy." https://www.churchofjesuschrist.org/study/scriptures/gs/blaspheme-blasphemy?lang=eng.

Clement. *Quis Dives Salvetur*. In *ANF* 2:591–604.

———. *Stromata, or Miscellanies*. In *ANF* 2:299–567.

Commodianus. *Instructions in Favour of Christian Discipline*. In *ANF* 4:203–18.

Coniaris, Anthony M. *These Are the Sacraments: The Life-Giving Mysteries of the Orthodox Church*. Minneapolis: Light & Life, 1981.

Connolly, R. Hugh, ed. *Didascalia Apostolorum: The Syriac Version Translated and Accompanied by the Verona Latin Fragments*. Oxford: Clarendon, 1929.

Cooper, Jordan B. "Bishops and Apostolic Succession in the Early Church." Dr. Jordan B. Cooper, Dec. 1, 2020. YouTube video, 13:29. https://www.youtube.com/watch?v=7fn9p2VT64Q.

———. "On Apostolic Succession." Dr. Jordan B. Cooper, Jan. 30, 2019. YouTube video, 7:59. https://www.youtube.com/watch?v=2xRwwCswp1I.

Council of Ancyra. *Canons*. In *NPNF* 2 14:63–75.

Council of Arles. "The *Canons* from the Council of Arles (A.D. 314)." Fourth-Century Christianity. https://www.fourthcentury.com/arles-314-canons/.

Council of Elvira. *Canons*. In *Morality and Ethics in Early Christianity*, edited and translated by Jan Womer, 75–82. Philadelphia: Fortress, 1987. https://web.archive.org/web/20120716202800/http://faculty.cua.edu/pennington/Canon%20Law/ElviraCanons.htm.

Council of Laodicea. *Canons*. In *NPNF* 2 14:[125]–34.

Council of Neocaesarea in Pontus. *Canons*. In *NPNF* 2 14:79–86.

Cyprian. *Epistulae, or Letters*. In *ANF* 5:267–409.

———. *On the Dress of Virgins*. In *ANF* 5:430–36.

———. *On the Lord's Prayer*. In *ANF* 5:447–57.

———. *On the Lapsed*. In *ANF* 5:437–47.

———. *On Works and Alms*. In *ANF* 5:476–84.

———. *To Antonianus, on Cornelius and Novatian, Epistle* 55. In *Opera omnia* 3, edited by Wilhelm August Hartel, 624–48. Corpus scriptorum ecclesiasticorum latinorum 2. Vienna: Geroldi, 1868.

Cyprian and Council of Sixty-Six Bishops. "Epistle." In *ANF* 5:353–54.

Cyprian and Second Council of Carthage. "Epistle to Cornelius, Concerning Granting Peace to the Lapsed." In *ANF* 5:336–38.

Cyril. *Catechetical Lectures of S. Cyril, Archbishop of Jerusalem*. In *NPNF* 2 7:1–157.

———. *The Works of Saint Cyril of Jerusalem*. 2 vols. Translated by P. McCauley and Anthony A. Stephenson. Washington, DC: Catholic University of America Press, 1969.

Daley, Brian E. *Gregory of Nazianzus*. London: Routledge, 2006.

Dallen, James. *The Reconciling Community: The Rite of Penance*. New York: Pueblo, 1986.

Dallen, James, and Joseph A. Favazza. *Removing the Barriers: The Practice of Reconciliation*. Chicago: Liturgy Training, 1991.

Daly, C. B. "Novatian and Tertullian." *Irish Theological Quarterly* 19:1 (1952) 33–43.

DelCogliano, Mark, et al. *Works on the Spirit: Athanasius's Letters to Serapion on the Holy Spirit, and, Didymus's On the Holy Spirit*. Yonkers, NY: St. Vladimir's Seminary Press, 2011.

Detisch, Scott. "A Brief History of the Sacrament of Reconciliation." https://frbenokala.com/wp-content/uploads/2024/04/Brief-History-of-the-Sacrament-of-Reconciliation.pdf.

Didache, or Teaching of the Twelve Apostles. In *ANF* 7:377–82.

Didymus. *Commentary on Genesis*. Translated by Robert C. Hill. Washington, DC: Catholic University of America Press, 2016.

———. *Commentary on Zechariah*. Translated by Robert C. Hill. Washington, DC: Catholic University of America Press, 2005.

———. *On the Holy Spirit*. In *Works on the Spirit: Athanasius's Letters to Serapion on the Holy Spirit, and, Didymus's* On the Holy Spirit, edited by Mark DelCogliano et al., 143–228. Yonkers, NY: St. Vladimir's Seminary Press, 2011.

Dionysius. "Epistle to Novatus" [Novatian]. In *ANF* 6:97.

———. "Epistle to Philemon, a Presbyter of Bishop Sixtus of Rome." In *ANF* 6:102–3.

———. "Letter to Conon." In *St. Dionysius of Alexandria: Letters and Treatises*, edited and translated by Charles Lett Feltoe. London: Society for Promoting Christian Knowledge, [1918].

———. "Letter to Fabius, Bishop of Antioch." In *ANF* 6:97–101.

———. *On the Reception of the Lapsed to Penitence*. In *ANF* 6:120 (exegetical fragment VII).

Doran, Thomas G. "On the Sacrament of Penance or Reconciliation." EWTN, 1999. https://www.ewtn.com/catholicism/library/doing-penance-3818.

Dudley, Martin, and Geoffrey Rowell. *Confession and Absolution*. Collegeville, MN: Liturgical, 1990.

Duffy, Edward F. "The Tura Papyrus of Didymus the Blind's Commentary on Job: An Original Translation with Introduction and Commentary." PhD diss., Graduate Theological Foundation, Donaldson, IN, 2000.

Dunkle, Brian P. "Gregory Nazianzen's Poems on Scripture: Introduction, Translation, and Commentary." STL diss., Weston Jesuit Faculty of the Boston College School of Theology and Ministry, 2009.

Ehrhardt, Arnold. *The Apostolic Succession in the First Two Centuries of the Church*. London: Lutterworth, 1953.

Elliott, J. K. "Is Postbaptismal Sin Forgivable?" *Bible Translator* 28.3 (1977) 330–32.

Encyclopedia.com. "Severian of Gabala." https://www.encyclopedia.com/religion/encyclopedias-almanacs-transcripts-and-maps/severian-gabala.

Ephrem. *Ephrem the Syrian: Hymns*. Translated by Kathleen E. McVey. New York: Paulist, 1989.

———. *The Hymns on Faith*. Translated by Jeffrey T. Wickes. Washington, DC: Catholic University of America Press, 2015.

———. "Rhythm Against the Jews, Delivered upon Palm Sunday." In *Selected Works of S. Ephrem the Syrian*, translated by J. B. Morris, [61]–83. London: Rivington, 1847.

———. *Selected Prose Works: Commentary on Genesis, Commentary on Exodus, Homily on Our Lord, Letter to Publius*. Translated by Edward G. Mathews. Washington, DC: Catholic University of America Press, 1994.

———. *S. Ephraim's Prose Refutations of Mani, Marcion, and Bardaisan: Transcribed from the Palimpsest B. M. Add 14623*. Translated by C. W. Mitchell. England: Gregg International, 1969.

———. *Songs for the Fast and Pascha*. Translated by Blake Hartung. Paris: Catholic University of America Press, 2023.

Eusebius of Cesaerea. *Against Marcellus and On Ecclesiastical History*. Translated by Kelly Spoerl and Markus Vinzent. Washington, DC: Catholic University of America Press, 2017.

———. *Church History*. Translated by Arthur Cushman McGiffert. In *NPNF* 2 1:[1]–387.

———. *Commentary on Isaiah*. Edited by Joel C. Elowsky. Translated by Jonathan J. Armstrong. Westmont, IL: InterVarsity, 2013.

Eusebius of Emesa. *On Repentance*. Translated by Roger Pearse. https://www.roger-pearse.com/weblog/wp-content/uploads/2023/07/Eusebius-of-Emesa-On-Repentance.pdf.

Evagrius. *On Thoughts*. In *Evagrius of Pontus: The Greek Ascetic Corpus*, translated by Robert E. Sinkewicz, 153–82. Oxford: Oxford University Press, 2003.

Ferguson, Everett. "Early Church Penance." *Restoration Quarterly* 36 (1994) [81]–100.

———, ed. *Encyclopedia of Early Christianity*. New York: Garland, 1990.

Fier, Don. "The History of the Sacrament Of Penance." *Wanderer*, June 17, 2017. https://thewandererpress.com/catholic/news/our-catholic-faith/the-history-of-the-sacrament-of-penance/.

First Council of Constantinople. *Canons and Synodal Letters*. In *NPNF* 2 14:170–89.

First Council of Nicaea. *Canons*. In *NPNF* 2 14:8–42.

First Epistle of Clement. In *ANF* 1:[5]–21 and 10:[229]–48.

Firth, Francis. "Bishops and Reconciliation—1." *Canadian Catholic Review* 10.7 (1992) 33–34.

———. "Bishops and Reconciliation—2." *Canadian Catholic Review* 10.8 (1992) 35–36.

———. "Saint Cyprian: Repentance After Baptism." *Canadian Catholic Review* 12.9 (1994) 38–40.

Fitzgerald, Allan D. "Innocent I: Insight into the History of Penance." *Revue d'Etudes Augustiniennes et Patristiques* 54.1 (2008) 95–110.

Fitzgerald, Paul Joseph. "A Model for Dialogue: Cyprian of Carthage on Ecclesial Discernment." *Theological Studies* 59.2. (1998) 236–53.

———. "Penance." In *The Oxford Handbook of Early Christian Studies*, edited by Susan Ashbrook Harvey and David G. Hunter, 786–807. Oxford Handbooks. Oxford: Oxford University Press, 2008.

Formula of Concord: Solid Declaration. 1577. In *Book of Concord: Triglot Concordia: The Symbolical Books of the Evangelical Lutheran Church, German-Latin-English*. St. Louis: Concordia, 1921.

Fourth-Century Christianity. "Early Christian Councils." May 1, 2025. https://www.fourthcentury.com/councils-and-creeds/.

Frend, William H. C. *The Early Church*. Minneapolis: Fortress, 1982.

———. *Saints and Sinners in the Early Church: Differing and Conflicting Traditions in the First Six Centuries*. Wilmington, DL: Glazier, 1985.

Geerard, Maurice. *Clavis Patrum Graecorum*. Turnhout, Belgium: Brepols, 1974.

Gilbert, Peter. *On God and Man: The Theological Poetry of St. Gregory of Nazianzus*. Crestwood, NY: St. Vladimir's Seminary Press, 2001.

Goehring, James E. *The Letter of Ammon and Pachomian Monasticism*. Berlin: De Gruyter, 1986.

Greer, Rowan A., and J. Warren Smith. *One Path for All: Gregory of Nyssa on the Christian Life and Human Destiny*. Eugene, OR: Cascade, 2015.

Gregory of Nazianzus. *Carmina Theologica A*. In *Patrologiae Cursus Completus: Series Graeca*, vol. 37, edited by Jacques-Paul Migne, cols. 929–930. Paris: Imprimerie Catholique, 1862.

———. *Funeral Oration on His Father*. In *Funeral Orations*, written by Ambrose and Gregory of Nazianzus, translated by Leo P. McCauley, 119–56. Baltimore: Catholic University of America Press, 1953.

———. *Gregory of Nazianzus's Letter Collection: The Complete Translation*. Translated by Bradley K. Storin. Oakland: University of California Press, 2019.

———. "Hymn to Parthenie (II.1.2.1–214) Christianizing Greek Theogonies." In *Poetry, Bible and Theology from Late Antiquity to the Middle Ages*, edited by Michele Cutino, translated by Miguel Herrero de Jáuregui, [259]–71. Berlin: de Gruyter, 2020.

———. *Orations*. In *NPNF* 2 7:423–853.

———. *Three Poems*. Edited by Thomas P. Halton. Translated by Denis Molaise Meehan. Washington DC: Catholic University of America Press, 1987.

Gregory of Nazianzus and Ambrose. *Funeral Orations by Saint Gregory Nazianzen and Saint Ambrose.* Translated by Leo P. McCauley et al. Baltimore: Catholic University of America Press, 1953.

Gregory of Nyssa. *Answer to Eunomius' Second Book.* In *NPNF* 2 5:478–587.

———. *Ascetical Works.* Translated by Virginia Woods Callahan. Washington, DC: Catholic University of America Press, 1999. ProQuest Ebook Central.

———. *Canonical Epistle to Letoius, Bishop of Melitine.* In *The Penitential Discipline of the Primitive Church for the First Four Hundred Years After Christ, Together with Its Declension from the Fifth Century, Downwards to Its Present State: Impartially Represented*, edited by Nathaniel Marshall, [185]–98. New ed. Oxford: John Henry Parker, 1844.

———. *Funeral Oration on Meletius.* In *NPNF* 2 5:963–72.

———. *The Great Catechism.* In *NPNF* 2 5:874–961.

———. *Homilies on Ecclesiastes: An English Version with Supporting Studies.* Edited by Stuart G. Hall. Berlin: De Gruyter, 1993.

———. *Homilies on the Beatitudes: An English Version with Supporting Studies.* Edited by Hubertus R. Drobner and Alberto Viciano. Boston: Brill, 2000.

———. *Homilies on the Song of Songs.* Atlanta: SBL, 2012. ProQuest Ebook Central.

———. *Letters: Introduction, Translation, and Commentary.* Translated by Anna M. Silvas. Leiden: Brill, 2006.

———. *The Life of Moses.* Edited and translated by Abraham J. Malherbe and Everett Ferguson. New York: Paulist, 1978.

———. *On Infants' Early Deaths.* In *NPNF* 2 5:692–708.

———. *On the Baptism of Christ.* In *NPNF* 2 5:973–84.

———. *On the Faith.* LibriVox recording, 11:07. https://ia601807.us.archive.org/3/items/theearlychurchcollection_volume_1_2102_librivox/ecc01_07_onthefaith_gregorynyssa_128kb.mp3.

———. *On the Holy Spirit, Against the Followers of Macedonius.* In *NPNF* 2 5:315–22.

———. *On the Holy Trinity, and of the Godhead of the Holy Spirit.* LibriVox recording, 20:41. https://ia601807.us.archive.org/3/items/theearlychurchcollection_volume_1_2102_librivox/ecc01_01_holytrinity_gregorynyssa_64kb.mp3.

———. *On the Life and Wonders of Our Father Among the Saints, Gregory the Wonderworker.* In *St. Gregory Thaumaturgus: Life and Works*, translated by Michael Slusser, 41–87. Washington, DC: Catholic University of America Press, 1998.

———. *On the Making of Man.* In *NPNF* 2 5:716–97.

———. *On the Six Days of Creation.* Philadelphia: Catholic University of America Press, 2021. ProQuest Ebook Central.

———. *On the Soul and the Resurrection.* In *NPNF* 2 5:801–78.

Gregory Thaumaturgus. *Canonical Epistle.* In *ANF* 6:18–20.

Hägerland, Tobias. *Jesus and the Forgiveness of Sins: An Aspect of His Prophetic Mission.* Cambridge: Cambridge University Press, 2011. ProQuest Ebook Central.

Halliburton, John. "'A Godly Discipline': Penance in the Early Church." In *Confession and Absolution*, edited by Martin Dudley and Geoffrey Rowell, 40–55. Collegeville, MN: Liturgical, 1990.

Hallock, Frank H., trans. "Aphraates on Penitents." *Journal of the Society of Oriental Research* 16 (1932) 43–56. https://www.tertullian.org/fathers/aphrahat_dem7.htm.

Hanson, Craig L. *Iberian Fathers: Pacian of Barcelona and Orosius of Braga.* Washington, DC: Catholic University of America Press, 1999.

Harris, Carl Vernon. *Origen of Alexandria's Interpretation of the Teacher's Function in the Early Christian Hierarchy and Community.* New York: American, 1966.

Harvey, Susan Ashbrook, and David G. Hunter. *The Oxford Handbook of Early Christian Studies.* Oxford Handbooks. Oxford: Oxford University Press, 2008.

Haslehurst, R. S. T. *Some Account of the Penitential Discipline of the Early Church in the First Four Centuries.* London: SPCK, 1921.

Hein, Kenneth. *Eucharist and Excommunication: A Study in Early Christian Doctrine and Discipline.* 2nd ed. Bern, Switzerland: Herbert Lang, 1975.

Heine, Ronald E., ed. *Gregory of Nyssa's Treatise on the Inscriptions of the Psalms.* Oxford: Oxford University Press, 1995. ProQuest Ebook Central.

Hilary. *Commentary on Matthew.* Translated by D. H. Williams. Washington, DC: Catholic University of America Press, 2013.

———. *De Synodis, or On the Councils.* In *NPNF* 2 9:4–29.

———. *De Trinitate, or On the Trinity.* In *NPNF* 2 9:40–233.

Hippolytus. *Against Noetus.* In *ANF* 5:223–31.

———. "The *Apostolic Tradition* of Hippolytus." Biblicalia. https://www.bombaxo.com/hippolytus-the-apostolic-tradition/.

———. *Commentary on Daniel.* Translated by Thomas Coffman Schmidt. https://www.pergrazia.com/wp-content/uploads/2019/12/0205_hippolytus_commentary-on-daniel_2010.pdf.

———. *Philosophumena, or Against Heresies.* In *ANF* 5:9–153.

———. *The Treatise on the Apostolic Tradition of St. Hippolytus of Rome, Bishop, and Martyr.* Edited by Gregory Dix and Henry Chadwick. London: SPCK, 1968.

Ignatius. "Letter to the Philadelphians." In *ANF* 1:75–89.

"Individual Confession and Forgiveness." In *Evangelical Lutheran Worship*, 243–44. Minneapolis: Augsburg Fortress, 2006.

"Individual Confession and Forgiveness." In *Lutheran Book of Worship*, 196–97. Minneapolis: Augsburg, 1978.

Irenaeus. *Against Heresies.* In *ANF* 1:315–567.

Jerome. *Commentaries on Galatians, Titus, and Philemon.* Translated by Thomas P. Scheck. Notre Dame, IN: University of Notre Dame Press, 2010.

———. *Commentary on Ecclesiastes*. Translated by Richard J. Goodrich and David Miller. New York: Newman, 2012.

———. *Dialogue Against the Luciferians*. In *NPNF* 2 6:728–757.

———. *Letters of Saint Jerome*. In *NPNF* 2 6:1–296.

———. *Life of Malchus, the Captive Monk*. In *NPNF* 2 6:722–27.

———. *Life of Paulus, the First Hermit*. In *NPNF* 2 6:695–701.

———. *Life of S. Hilarion*. In *NPNF* 2 6:702–21.

———. *On Illustrious Men*. Washington, DC: Catholic University of America Press, 1999.

———. *Prefaces to Jerome's Early Works*. In *NPNF* 2 6:1030–43.

———. *Perpetual Virginity of Blessed Mary*. In *NPNF* 2 6:758–78.

John, Bishop of Constantinople. "Syriac Version of the Discourse of Mar John, Bishop of Constantinople, on Virginity, and Repentance, and Admonition." In *Coptic Homilies in the Dialect of Upper Egypt*, translated by Ernest Alfred Wallis Budge, [337]–79. London: British Museum, 1910.

Johnson, Nancy Elizabeth. "Living Death: Baptism and the Christian Life in the Writings of Basil of Caesarea, Gregory of Nazianzus, and Gregory of Nyssa." PhD diss., University of Notre Dame, 2008.

Joyce, G. H. "Private Penance in the Early Church." *Journal of Theological Studies* 42.165/166 (1941) 18–42.

Justin Martyr. *Dialogue with Trypho*. In *ANF* 1:194–270.

Kantiotes, Augustinos N. "The Benefits of the Mystery." In *On the Divine Liturgy, Orthodox Homilies*, vol. 2, translated by Asterios Gerostergios, [208]–11. Belmont, MA: Institute for Byzantine and Modern Greek Studies, 1986.

Kerns, Loren. "Tertullian and the Catechumenate: An Inquiry into Tertullian's Justification for the North African Catechumenate in the Early Third Century." MAT thesis, George Fox Evangelical Seminary, 2000.

Kimball, Edward L. "Confession in LDS Doctrine and Practice." In *Brigham Young University Studies* 36.2 (1996) 7–73. http://www.jstor.org/stable/43041988.

Lactantius. *Divine Institutes*. In *ANF* 7:9–255.

Landon, Edward H. *A Manual of Councils of the Holy Catholic Church*. New and revised ed. Edinburgh: J. Grant, 1909.

Larsen, Matthew, and Michael Svigel. "The First Century Two Ways Catechesis and Hebrews 6:1–6." In *The Didache: A Missing Piece of the Puzzle in Early Christianity*, edited by Jonathan A. Draper and Clayton N. Jefford, 477–96. Atlanta: SBL, 2015.

Lehto, Adam Isaac. "Divine Law, Asceticism, and Gender in Aphrahat's '*Demonstrations*,' with a Complete Annotated Translation of the Text." PhD diss., University of Toronto, 2003.

Litke, Austin Dominic. "Translator's Introduction: Homily 16 on 'In the Beginning Was the Word' by St. Basil of Caesarea." *Logos: A Journal of Catholic Thought & Culture* 26 (2023) 148–50. doi:10.1353/log.2023.0016.

Logan, Alastair H. B. "Marcellus of Ancyra (Pseudo-Anthimus), 'On the Holy Church': Text, Translation and Commentary." *Journal of Theological Studies* 51.1 (2000) 81–112.

Luther, Martin. *Luther's Works: Word and Sacrament 1*. Edited by E. Theodore Bachmann. Philadelphia: Muhlenberg, 1960.

Maas, Korey D. "TGC 047—Apostolic Succession." Gottesdienst Online, July 10, 2019. YouTube video, 57:32. https://www.youtube.com/watch?=Fmt5AOxuaaCU.

Macé, Caroline, et al, trans. "De Beneficentia: A Homily on Social Action Attributed to Basil." *Vigiliae Christianae* 66.5 (2012) 457–81. http://www.jstor.org/stable/41722515.

Marshall, Christopher D. "Repentance." In *The Oxford Encyclopedia of the Bible and Theology*. Oxford: Oxford University Press, 2014.

Marshall, Nathaniel. *The Penitential Discipline of the Primitive Church, for the First 400 Years After Christ: Together with Its Declension from the Fifth Century Downwards to Its Present State, Impartially Represented*. London: Printed for W. Taylor and H. Clements, 1714.

Martin, Ralph P., and Peter H. Davids, eds. *Dictionary of the Later New Testament and Its Developments: A Compendium of Contemporary Biblical Scholarship*. Westmont, IL: InterVarsity, 1997.

Martyrdom of Pionius. In *The Acts of the Christian Martyrs*, translated by Herbert Musurillo, 136–67. Oxford: Clarendon, 1972.

Mateo-Seco, Lucas Francisco, and Giulio Maspero. *The Brill Dictionary of Gregory of Nyssa: Supplements to Vigiliae Christianae*. Leiden: Brill, 2010.

Maynard-Reid, P. U. "Forgiveness." In *Dictionary of the Later New Testament and Its Developments: A Compendium of Contemporary Biblical Scholarship*, edited by Ralph P. Martin and Peter H. Davids, 379–82. Westmont, IL: InterVarsity, 1997.

McCarthy, Carmel, trans. "Saint Ephrem's Commentary on Tatian's *Diatessaron*: An English Translation of Chester Beatty Syriac MS 709." *Journal of Semitic Studies Supplement* 2. Oxford: Oxford University Press, 1993.

McDonnell, Kilian. "Communion Ecclesiology and Baptism in the Spirit: Tertullian and the Early Church." *Theological Studies* 49 (1988) 671–94.

McHugh, Michael P. "Commodian." In *Encyclopedia of Early Christianity*, edited by Everett Ferguson, 222. New York: Garland, 1990.

McNamara, Kevin. "Penance: Sacrament of Reconciliation." *Furrow* 36.1 (1985) 3–17. http://www.jstor.org/stable/27677993.

Methodius. "On Leprosy—An Allegorical Explanation of Leviticus 13 (*De Lepra ad Sistelium*)." Translated by Ralph Cleminson and Andrew Eastbourne. 2015. https://www.roger-pearse.com/weblog/wp-content/uploads/2015/09/Methodius-De-Lepra-20151.pdf.

Mitchell, Margaret M. *The Heavenly Trumpet: John Chrysostom and the Art of Pauline Interpretation*. Louisville: Westminster John Knox, 2002.

———. *John Chrysostom on Paul: Praises and Problem Passages*. Atlanta: SBL, 2022.

Mokhoathi, Joel. "Christian Piety and Pardon: The Vindication of Postbaptismal Sins." *Pharos Journal of Theology* 99 (2018) 1–12.

Morrisey, Francis G. "The Apostolic Succession of the Canadian Latin Rite Bishops." *Studia canonica* 6.2 (1972) 315–48.

Mortimer, R. C. *The Origins of Private Penance in the Western Church*. Oxford: Clarendon, 1939.

Murphy, Edwina. "Divine Ordinances and Life-Giving Remedies: Galatians in the Writings of Cyprian of Carthage." *Journal of Theological Interpretation* 8.1 (2014) 81–101.

New Advent. "Sacrament of Penance." https://www.newadvent.org/cathen/11618c.htm.

Novatian. *On the Trinity*. In *ANF* 5:611–44.

On the Glory of Martyrdom. In *ANF* 5:529–87.

Origen. *Against Celsus*. In *ANF* 4:395–669.

———. *Commentary of Origen on the Gospel of St. Matthew*. 2 vols. Translated by Ronald E. Heine. Oxford: Oxford University Press, 2018.

———. *Commentary on John*. In *ANF* 10:297–408.

———. *Commentary on the Gospel of John, Books 1–10*. Translated by Ronald E. Heine. Washington, DC: Catholic University of America Press, 1989.

———. *Commentary on the Gospel of John, Books 13–32*. Translated by Ronald E. Heine. Washington, DC: Catholic University of America Press, 1993.

———. *Commentary on Matthew*. In *ANF* 10:413–512.

———. *Commentary on Romans*. 2 vols. Translated by Thomas P. Scheck. Washington, DC: Catholic University of America Press, 2001–2002.

———. *Exhortation to Martyrdom, or Exhortatio ad Martyrium*. In *Alexandrian Christianity: Selected Translations of Clement and Origen*, translated by John Ernest Leonard Oulton and Henry Chadwick, 388–429. London: SCM, 1954.

———. *Homilies (or Commentary) on First Corinthians*. Unpublished translation.

———. *Homilies 1–14 on Ezekiel*. Translated by Thomas P. Scheck. Mahwah, NJ: Newman, 2010.

———. *Homilies on Jeremiah*. Translated by John Clark Smith. Washington, DC: Catholic University of America Press, 1998.

———. *Homilies on Joshua*. Edited by Cynthia White. Translated by Barbara J. Bruce. Washington, DC: Catholic University of America Press, 2002.

———. *Homilies on Leviticus*. Translated by Gary Wayne Barkley. Washington, DC: Catholic University of America Press, 1990.

———. *Homilies on Luke; Fragments on Luke*. Translated by Joseph T. Lienhard. Washington, DC: Catholic University of America Press, 1996.

———. *Homilies on Numbers*. Edited by Christopher A. Hall. Translated by Thomas P. Scheck. Downers Grove, IL: IVP Academic, 2009.

———. *Homilies on Psalm 37*. In *Homélies sur les Psaumes 36 à 38*, translated by Henri Crouzel and Luc Brésard, 257–327. Paris: Cerf, 1995.

———. *Homilies on the Psalms: Codex Monacensis Graecus 314*. Translated by Joseph Wilson Trigg. Washington, DC: Catholic University of America Press, 2020.

———. *On First Principles, or De principiis*. In *ANF* 4:239–382.

———. *On Prayer*. In *Patrologia graeca*, vol. 11, edited by Jean Paul Migne, translated by William A. Curtis, cols. 529–30. Paris: Apud Garnier Fratres, 1862. https://ccel.org/ccel/origen/prayer/prayer.i.html.

Oulton, John Ernest Leonard, and Henry Chadwick, eds. *Alexandrian Christianity: Selected Translations*. Philadelphia: Westminster, 1954.

Pacian. *Letters* [to Sympronian]. In *Iberian Fathers: Pacian of Barcelona and Orosius of Braga*, translated by Craig L. Hanson, 17–70. Washington, DC: Catholic University of America Press, 1999.

———. *On Penitents*. In *Iberian Fathers: Pacian of Barcelona and Orosius of Braga*, translated by Craig L. Hanson, 71–86. Washington, DC: Catholic University of America Press, 1999.

Palmer, Paul F. *Sacraments and Forgiveness: History and Doctrinal Development of Penance, Extreme Unction and Indulgences*. Westminster, MD: Newman, 1959.

Pasquato, Ottorino. "Catechumenate—Discipleship." In *Encyclopedia of Ancient Christianity*, edited by Angelo Di Berardino, 1:457–71. Downers Grove, IL: IVP Academic, 2014.

Pastor of Hermas. In *ANF* 2:9–55.

Percer, Leo R. "Confidence in Christ and the Sin unto Death—When Should a Believer Not Pray? 1 John 5:13–21." *Eruditio Ardescens* 1.2 (2014) 1–21. https://digitalcommons.liberty.edu/jlbts/vol1/iss2/7.

Peter of Alexandria. *Canonical Epistle*. In *ANF* 6:269–79.

Philostorgius. *Church History*. Translated by Philip R. Amidon. Writings From the Greco-Roman World. Atlanta: SBL, 2007.

Poschmann, Bernhard. *Penance and the Anointing of the Sick*. Translated by Francis Courtney. Eugene, OR: Wipf & Stock, 2018.

Quasten, Johannes. *Patrology*. 4 vols. Westminster, MD: Christian Classics, 1986.

Rahner, Karl. *Penance in the Early Church*. Translated by Lionel Swain. New York: Crossroad, 1982.

Ramsey, Boniface. *Beginning to Read the Fathers*. New York: Paulist, 1985.

Reddit. "Justification Covering Postbaptismal Sins." r/Reformed. https://www.reddit.com/r/Reformed/comments/k78kpc/justification_covering_postbaptismal_sins/.

Reilly, William L. "The Outlook of St. Basil on Pagan Literature in His Address to Young Men on Greek Literature." MA diss., Department of Classics at Fordham University, 1940.

Rodden, John. "How the Irish Changed Penance: The History of a Sacrament." *Commonweal*, Feb. 14, 2022. https://www.commonwealmagazine.org/how-irish-changed-penance.

Roitto, Rikard. "Rituals of Reintegration." In *The Oxford Handbook of Early Christian Ritual*, edited by Rikard Roitto et al., 436–43. Oxford Handbooks Online. New York: Oxford University Press, 2019.

Schwartz, Daniel L. *Paideia and Cult: Christian Initiation in Theodore of Mopsuestia*. Hellenic Studies Series 57. Washington, DC: Center for Hellenic Studies, 2013. http://nrs.harvard.edu/urn-3:hul.ebook:CHS_SchwartzD.Paideia_and_Cult.2013.

Scott, Colby A. "A Translation of Four Verse Homilies of Reproof Attributed to Saint Ephrem the Syrian." In *St. Ephrem the Syrian's Spiritual Guidance: A Study of the Verse Homilies on Reproof*, 138–325. PhD diss., School of Arts and Sciences of the Catholic University of America, 2020.

Senn, Frank C. "Structures of Penance and the Ministry of Reconciliation." *Lutheran Quarterly* 25.3 (1973) 270–83.

Severian. "A Most Beneficial Sermon on Faith, and About the Law of Nature, and on the Holy Spirit (De fide et de lege natura)." Translated by Bryson Sewell. 2014. https://www.roger-pearse.com/weblog/wp-content/uploads/2014/06/Severian-of-Gabala-A-most-beneficial-sermon-on-faith-and-about-the-law-of-nature-and-on-the-holy-spirit-tr-Bryson-Sewell.pdf.

———. "Sermon on the Epiphany." In "Notes on a Text by Severian of Gabala," written by Peter Gilbert. *De unione ecclesiarum* (blog), Apr. 7, 2010. https://bekkos.wordpress.com/2010/04/07/notes-on-a-text-by-severian-of-gabala/.

———. "Severian of Gabala De Sacrificiis Caini (PG 62: 719–722 = CPG 4208): Draft Translation." Translated by K. P. Academia, n.d. https://www.academia.edu/13020533/Severian_of_Gabala_De_Sacrificiis_Caini_PG_62_719_722_CPG_4208_Draft_Translation.

Severian and Bede. *Commentaries on Genesis 1–3: Severin of Gabala and Bede the Venerable*. Edited by Michael Glerup. Downers Grove, IL: IVP Academic, 2010.

Sider, Robert D. "Cyprian." In *Encyclopedia of Early Christianity*, edited by Everett Ferguson, 246–49. New York: Garland, 1990.

Silvas, Anna M. *Basil of Caesarea: Questions of the Brothers*. Leiden: Brill, 2014.

Sinkewicz, Robert E. *Evagrius of Pontus: The Greek Ascetic Corpus*. Oxford: Oxford University Press, 2003.

Slusser, Michael, ed. *Life and Works by Saint Gregory Thaumaturgus*. Washington, DC: Catholic University of America Press, 1998.

Socrates Scholasticus. *Ecclesiastical History*. From *Nicene and Post-Nicene Fathers*, second series, vol. 2, edited by Philip Schaff and Henry Wace, translated by A. C. Zenos. Buffalo, NY: Christian Literature, 1890. Revised and edited for New Advent by Kevin Knight. https://www.newadvent.org/fathers/2601.htm.

Sorabji, Richard. *Moral Conscience Through the Ages Fifth Century BCE to the Present*. Chicago: University of Chicago Press, 2014.

Sozomen, Salaminius Hermias. "Ecclesiastical History." From *Nicene and Post-Nicene Fathers*, second series, vol. 2, edited by Philip Schaff and Henry Wace, translated by Chester D. Hartranft. Buffalo, NY: Christian Literature, 1890. Revised and edited for New Advent by Kevin Knight. https://www.newadvent.org/fathers/2602.htm.

Swanston, Hamish. "Penance and the History of Penance." *New Blackfriars* 50.594 (1969) 754–59.

Swete, H. B. "Penitential Discipline in the First Three Centuries." *Journal of Theological Studies* 4.15 (1903) 321–37. https://doi.org/10.1093/jts/os-IV.15.321.

Tanghe, D. A. "L'Eucharistie pour la rémission des péchés." *Irénikon* 34 (1961) 165–81.

Tatian. *The Diatessaron*. In *ANF* 10:43–129.

Tertullian. *Against Marcion*. In *ANF* 3:[271]–474.

———. *De praescriptione haereticorum, or The Prescription against Heretics*. In *ANF* 3:243–65.

———. *On Modesty*. In *ANF* 4:74–101.

———. *On Repentance*. In *ANF* 3:[657]–66.

———. *To the Martyrs*. In *ANF* 3:[693]–96.

Testimonies Against the Jews. In *ANF* 5:507–57.

Theodore. *Commentaries on the Minor Epistles of Paul*. Translated by Rowan A. Greer. Atlanta: SBL, 2010.

———. *Commentary on Psalms 1–81*. Translated by Robert C. Hill. Atlanta: SBL, 2006.

———. *Commentary on the Gospel of John*. Translated by Joel C. Elowsky. Downers Grove, IL: IVP Academic, 2010.

———. *Commentary on the Nicene Creed*. Translated by Alphonse Mingana. Woodbrooke Studies 5. Cambridge, UK: W. Heffer, 1932.

———. *Commentary of Theodore of Mopsuestia on the Lord's Prayer and on the Sacraments of Baptism and the Eucharist*. Translated by Alphonse Mingana. Woodbrooke Studies 6. Cambridge, UK: W. Heffer, 1933.

———. *Commentary on the Twelve Prophets*. Translated by Robert C. Hill. Washington, DC: Catholic University of America Press, 2004.

Theognostus. *Seven Books of Hypotyposes or Outlines* [excerpts]. In *ANF* 6:155–56.

Theophilus I. "Coptic Homilies in the Dialect of Upper Egypt/Sermon 4: *Discourse of Our Holy Father, Apa Theophilos, the Archbishop, Which He Pronounced Concerning Repentance and Continence, and Also How a Man Must Not Neglect to Repent Before the Last Times Come Upon Him*." Wikisource. https://en.wikisource.org/wiki/Coptic_homilies_in_the_dialect_of_Upper_Egypt/Sermon_4.

Tipson, Baird. "A Dark Side of Seventeenth-Century English Protestantism: The Sin against the Holy Spirit." *Harvard Theological Review* 77.3/4 (1984) 301–30. http://www.jstor.org/stable/1509463.

Tsaftaridis, Ioannis. "Repentance and Confession: An Orthodox Perspective." *Pharos Journal of Theology* 98 (2017) 1–6.

Tsakiridis, George. "Addressing Guilt Within the Religious Community: Cyprian of Carthage, Reconciliation, and the Science of Emotion." *Theology and Science* 16.1 (2018) 92–106. https://doi.org/10.1080/14746700.2018.1416781.

Turner, Mark Joseph. "A History of Confession of Sin: From the Early Church to Modern Evangelicalism." *Reformed Theological Review* 79.1 (2020) 38–63.

Vivian, Tim. "The Good God, the Holy Power, and the Paraclete: Paraclete: of God (ad Filios Dei) by Saint Macarius the Great." *Anglican Theological Review* 80.3 (1998) 338–65.

von Campenhausen, Hans. *Ecclesiastical Authority and Spiritual Power in the Church of the First Three Centuries*. London: Adam & Charles Black, 1969.

Wagner, Nick. "Simple History of Reconciliation for RCIA Catechists." Team Initiation, June 2, 2013. https://teamrcia.com/2013/06/a-simple-history-of-reconciliation-for-rcia-catechists/.

Watkins, Oscar D. A. *History of Penance: Being a Study of the Authorities*. London: Longmans, Green, 1920.

White, L. Michael. "Penance." In *Encyclopedia of Early Christianity*, edited by Everett Ferguson, 708–11. New York: London: Garland, 1990.

Winner, Lauren F. *The Dangers of Christian Practice: On Wayward Gifts, Characteristic Damage, and Sin*. New Haven, CT: Yale University Press, 2018.

Womer, Jan L. *Morality and Ethics in Early Christianity*. Philadelphia: Fortress, 1987.

Young, Frances M., and Andrew Teal. *From Nicaea to Chalcedon: A Guide to the Literature and Its Background*. 2nd ed. Grand Rapids: Baker Academic, 2010.

Zins, Robert M. "The Blasphemy of the Holy Spirit, No Forgiveness in this Life or the Next Forever." Sermon Audio, May 5, 2020. 1:23:38. https://www.sermonaudio.com/solo/christiananswers/sermons/55205221256 07/.

Zuiddam, Benno A. "Repentance and Forgiveness: Classical and Patristic Perspectives on a Reformation Theme." *Skriflig* 56.1 (2022) a2813. https://doi.org/10.4102/ids.v56i1.2813.

www.ingramcontent.com/pod-product-compliance
Lightning Source LLC
LaVergne TN
LVHW020641100826
845148LV00012B/2275